3

ALSO BY ROBERT HASS

POETRY
Human Wishes
Praise
Field Guide

PROSE
Twentieth Century Pleasures

TRANSLATIONS
Provinces by Czeslaw Milosz (with Czeslaw Milosz)
The Collected Poems by Czeslaw Milosz (with Czeslaw Milosz et al.)
Unattainable Earth by Czeslaw Milosz (with Czeslaw Milosz)
The Separate Notebooks by Czeslaw Milosz (with Czeslaw Milosz, Robert
    Pinsky, and Renata Gorczynski)

ALSO BY STEPHEN MITCHELL

POETRY
Parables and Portraits

PROSE
The Gospel According to Jesus

TRANSLATIONS
Variable Directions: The Selected Poetry of Dan Pagis
Tao Te Ching
The Book of Job
The Selected Poetry of Yehuda Amichai (with Chana Bloch)
The Sonnets to Orpheus
The Lay of the Love and Death of Cornet Christoph Rilke
Letters to a Young Poet
The Notebooks of Malte Laurids Brigge
The Selected Poetry of Rainer Maria Rilke

ANTHOLOGIES
The Enlightened Mind: An Anthology of Sacred Prose
The Enlightened Heart: An Anthology of Sacred Poetry
Dropping Ashes on the Buddha: The Teaching of Zen Master Seung Sahn

INTO THE GARDEN:
A WEDDING ANTHOLOGY

INTO THE
GARDEN

A WEDDING ANTHOLOGY

Poetry and Prose on Love and Marriage

Edited by Robert Hass and Stephen Mitchell

HarperCollins *Publishers*

HarperCollins books may be purchased for educational, business, or
sales promotional use. For information, please write: Special Markets
Department, HarperCollins Publishers, Inc., 10 East 53rd Street,
New York, NY 10022.

Copyright acknowledgments can be found following page 197.

FIRST EDITION

Designed by David Bullen
Composition by Wilsted & Taylor

LIBRARY OF CONGRESS CATALOGING-IN-PUBLICATION DATA
Into the garden : a wedding anthology : poetry and prose on
    love and marriage / edited by Robert Hass and Stephen
    Mitchell.—1st ed.
        p.   cm.
    Includes index.
    ISBN 0-06-016919-2
    1. Weddings—Literary collections. 2. Love—Literary
collections. 3. Marriage—Literary collections. I. Hass,
Robert, 1941– . II. Mitchell, Stephen, 1943– .
PN6071.W4157   1993
808.8′0354—DC20   92-53339

93 94 95 96 97 RRD 10 9 8 7 6 5 4 3 2 1

To Brenda *To Vicki*

Contents

CEREMONIES

Foreword

Poets get asked so often by their friends and relatives to suggest appropriate readings for marriages that they come to be more aware than most people are of what a wedding is: a feast for the saying of a magic spell. A spell to call down to earth what we have sensed as divine love and to toss earthly love—like ribbons on the wind—into eternity, and to make that moment, its hopes and its bright intentions, hold through all the difficulties of a common life.

This magic is to be accomplished in a public ceremony so that the participants are seen to take responsibility for what they are saying. And it is accomplished in the gaze of a pair of lovers into each other's eyes, into the human depths (and the vastly complicated, largely unexplored terrain) of another person's soul while the central words are spoken. It is a saying and a binding: I, some person, take you, some person, for my . . .

And poets, with their heads full of old poems, hearing these words, are likely to hear also in the back of their minds an echo of some of the oldest magical language, the oldest scraps of poetry, on earth, when there was not much distinction between poetry and religious utterance, not much distinction between a prayer for good crops, for a friendly relation to the soil or the forest that feeds us, and a prayer for a young couple. At the beginning, the one was probably thought, in the way of all sympathetic magic, to depend on the other: you prayed for the marriage to be blessed as you prayed for the people to be blessed, as you prayed for the sun in its time and the rain in its time, as you prayed to the spirits of the animals you hunted, and to the fundamental magic of the green earth that renews itself and to the day and the year that renew themselves, and you prayed for this magic to be in the lovers and it in them. That old cry in the earliest Greek and Latin poetry remembered this history, and it was also a cry of spontaneous joy, a call to the feast:

> *O Hymenaee Hymen*
> *O Hymen Hymenaee*

It was in this spirit that Stephen Mitchell and I began this project. We had been asked for suggestions for poems so often in recent years that, talking about it, we began to feel that there was a need for a book like this. Not only because one didn't exist, but also because something has changed in the last decade or so in the way people think about weddings. It is not just that lovers about to be married want sacred words spoken on the occasion of their marriage—people have always wanted that—or even that they want the words to be somehow more personal to them than the usual wedding ceremony is, or to have an older deeper power, or more resonance. It is also that in our society the wedding is one of the few widely practiced, deeply traditional rituals, and it carries with it not only the steadying and magical power a tradition can give, it also brings into the present some of the baggage of the past that we'd like to be rid of, particularly where our sense of the sacred and of gender roles—of marriage as a meeting of two equal persons—are concerned.

Some couples love how deeply traditional a wedding is, some approach it with a certain irony, some with a slightly schizophrenic and perfectly natural combination of the two, a sense of longing and mystery on the one hand, and a wild sense of the comedy of what they are submitting themselves to on the other. But one way or another, a lot of couples feel that the traditions of the wedding ceremony as they have been passed from generation to generation need some sorting out, a winnowing of what they want to take from the past and what they don't. The simplest solution has seemed to be to add a few poems of their own choosing, poems that, inside the tradition, say something of what they want said about their love and the vows they are making, and how they understand their relation to each other.

The main purpose of this book is to help them in that task. We hope it will also help them to think about and to rethink the ceremony itself, and, of course, to think about marriage. And so we have included, as well as poems, some longer readings on the subject of love and marriage, some sample wedding ceremonies drawn from various American traditions, an essay on the marriage ceremony, and a brief afterword on marriage as a tao, a way in the world.

Weddings have traditionally belonged to women, probably because the world hasn't, and the male role has been in one way or another observer of or appendage to all the drama of planning. One of the ways men and women can reclaim their weddings as a common space is to think about their ceremony together. We hope this book will help in the work of making a new wedding, and of keeping the ancient power of the ceremony alive in the present.

R. H.

Poems and Weddings

Weddings, I have been thinking, have to do with a moment, and marriages have to do with time. As Stephen Mitchell and I read around and talked about this book, our main purpose was to try to find words that would help to deepen and enrich a ceremony, but of course we found ourselves talking and thinking and reading a lot of poems about love and marriage. And these three concerns suggested a shape for a useful introductory essay: first a word about love, then a brief history of the wedding ceremony, and then something about marriage and time.

Love first. Here is a little poem by Emily Dickinson, who never married, written probably when she was twenty-eight or twenty-nine years old:

> Wild Nights—Wild Nights!
> Were I with thee
> Wild Nights should be
> Our luxury!
>
> Futile—the Winds—
> To a Heart in port—
> Done with the Compass—
> Done with the Chart!
>
> Rowing in Eden—
> Ah, the Sea!
> Might I but moor—Tonight—
> In Thee!

I've just recently realized why this poem is so mysterious and beautiful to me. When you first read it, you get the impression that the speaker in the poem is throwing out the charts to navigate by the freedom of her feelings in the open sea. But it isn't so. She has thrown them out because she is in port, in safe harbor.

And that, I saw, is what we want from each other most intimately: wildness and safety, or a magical space that includes both. That is what it means to row in Eden. Dickinson herself came to believe, I think, that this dream-wedding was only possible in a passionate mind, which is to say in a poem. I don't think she thought you could have both in the real world. It's my experience that you can have both, not all of the time but some of the time, and that this possibility depends on the other more durable things that love means. And that the root of these is trust. Another poet, John Donne, described it this way in the sixteenth century:

> And now good morrow to our waking souls,
> Which watch not one another out of fear.

It means to live with eyes open, not fearing what you will see in the other person or what they will see in you. And that means, in turn, not hiding what might cause fear but showing it and seeing it through. The word for that quality in a person is "presence." None of us have a lot of it by the time we are adults because we've all learned, in order to get love, to hide what is unlovable in us. To unlearn that is risky and it takes time and it has to be done, in a marriage, while you are doing other things, making a living, living a life, raising children. The reason for doing it is that it is the only way to the dream-marriage we wanted at the moment of the wedding. And, as often happens, the process itself may turn out to be more surprising, may be a wilder and deeper thing than the dream. A wedding can't do this for us, of course, but it can express that intention clearly, for it too is a kind of poem, or at least, like a poem, it is a human invention to hold a kind of magic in place. And a wedding, unlike a poem, is partly a collective creation. Parts of it are designed by us, but mostly it is inherited from what others intended it to express. Which is why it seemed useful here to sketch a sort of history of the wedding ceremony.

Some friends were married recently. It was a large wedding in a very beautiful old Protestant church in Atlanta, and during the ceremony the minister, who seemed to some of us overstimulated by the splendor of the event, delivered himself of a twenty-minute sermon against divorce, conducted the rest of the ceremony rather gracefully, and at the end charged the groom with "leadership and strength of purpose" and the bride with "a quiet and submissive spirit."

Afterward one of our party claimed that he had also said that marriage was instituted by God to subdue lust and provide comfort in old age. None of the rest of us heard that, or perhaps we had let it go by, but it did make for amusement at the reception—which was gorgeous, full of sweet-smelling Southern flowers, and music, and tart, sparkling champagne—when we wondered what went on between the defeat of carnal appetite and the onset of senility. "Rituals of female submission," one bridesmaid suggested. The groom was of Scots-Irish stock, the bride of Chinese. The bridesmaid was African-American and she was the one who said, "The broomstick might have been better."

Which had a certain bitter force. During slavery, when couples were allowed to marry, the ritual in many places seems to have taken a particular form. A broomstick was placed down in the yard and the couple jumped over it. That was the marriage. I haven't been able to find out where or how this custom originated, but I found it moving, in a couple of ways: first of all, by contrast with the richly complicated West African wedding ceremonies I had been reading about, and second, because the human need for ritual is so deep that it had reasserted itself even in this simple form. There is some record of how the African (-becoming-American-the-hard-way) slaves felt about it. In my reading for this book I came across some verses, passed down, I guess, through the oral tradition, which are an ironic, probably outraged parody of a slave master's wedding speech:

> Dark an' stormy may come de wedder;
> I jines dis he-male and she-male togedder,
> Let none but Him dat makes de thunder,
> Put dis he-male and she-male asunder.
> I darfore 'nounce you bofe de same.
> Be good, go 'long, an' keep up yo' name.
> De broomstick's jumped, de worl's not wide.
> She's now yo' own. Salute yo' bride!

I also found it moving as an instance of how the human spirit survives the violence committed against it. The lesson of these two kinds of marriages, I guess, is that if you don't or can't attend to your ceremony and what it expresses, someone else will.

What gets expressed by our wedding ceremonies has very ancient roots, and some of our ways of thinking about marriage are, in human time, quite new. There are at least three assumptions in most of our marriages that evolved very gradually. They are that the partners are freely chosen, that they are getting married because they are in love, and that they are equal partners to the agreement. It wasn't always so.

I suppose it is always in the nature of tradition that we express some things with it and that much more gets expressed through it unconsciously. Thinking about weddings, I thought first of the model of *The Song of Songs*. I had assumed that sympathetic magic, sacred marriage, with its sense of the role of sexuality in nature and its celebration of the complementarity of the sexes and the fertility and beauty of the earth, was at the core of the festive ritual gesture of marriage. It may be so, but human marriages had first of all to do with families, and in most parts of the world they still do. Among most peoples and at most times marriage has been a practical arrangement between families to make a safe space for childbearing, to assure the protection and education of children, and, especially, to stabilize social alliances within the group. The social meaning of marriage is based not just on the fact that we yearn for a partner, but that, in order to get one, we need to marry out of our families. As a result, human society is constantly being disrupted and re-formed—we all seem to learn this at one time or another—by the energy of sexual attraction.

We can glimpse in this fact, at the beginning of social life, one of the most profound rhythms of all life, the interplay between stability and change. This is the deepest story—from the point of view of the group—of the weddings we now celebrate. They are the signal of a powerful change in the structure of a family, more powerful than either a death or the birth of a child, since they realign the group in relation to others in a way that those events do not. In this sense, among the central moments in the human cycle of birth, coming of age, marriage, and death, it is marriage that has the deepest social meaning. That's why marriages were arranged by families and why the desires of the individual were never the first consideration.

It is also the case that marriage emerged and developed from societies in which women had very little social and economic power. These societies were based on a conception of male authority and female consent that organized work and property. Religion was familial; it involved attention to the ancestors and the special gods of the household who watched over the family. So, probably, marriage emerged as a religious ritual, as a way of transferring the bride from the religion of her parents to the religion of her husband's family. Here is Fustel de Coulanges, a nineteenth-century French classical historian, on the origins of marriage in ancient Greece and Rome:

> Two families live side by side; but they have different gods. In one, a young daughter from her infancy takes a part in the religion of her father; she invokes his sacred fire; every day she offers it libations. She surrounds it with garlands and flowers on festal days. She asks its protection and returns thanks for its favors. This paternal fire is her god. Let a young man of neighboring family ask her in marriage, and something more is at stake than to pass from one house to another. She must abandon the paternal fire, and henceforth invoke that of her husband. She must abandon her religion, practice other rites. "From the hour of marriage," says one of the ancients, "the wife has no longer anything in common with the domestic religion of her fathers; she sacrifices at the hearth of her husband."

Marriage was a ritual of this domestic religion and it involved three parts. First, there was a ceremony in the bride's house, in which the father gives his daughter to the young man and makes a sacrifice to the hearth separating her from her family gods.

Second, there was a procession from the house of the father to the house of the husband. The bride usually travels in a cart or a chair borne by attendants. She is veiled and wears a crown. She is dressed in white, which was the color associated with all religious ritual. The senators of ancient Rome wore togas of pure white to the senate, and the color of their garments had a name, *candor*, from which one of our words for truthfulness comes. A torch preceded the bride, and songs were sung along the way. They usually called on the marriage god, Hymen, and the songs were called *hymeneals*. It was from these that the tradition of the epithalamion (song outside the bridal chamber) developed. As she entered her new home, the bride was careful not to step on the threshold, since she didn't belong to the family religion yet. Sometimes, in some cities, the whole procession was a feigned kidnapping, and young men carried the woman to her husband's house. Sometimes the husband simulated force at the threshold and carried the bride across.

In the third part of the ceremony, the bride is greeted by her new family and is introduced into its religion through prayers, a scattering of lustral water, and a touching of the sacred fire. Then husband and wife share a cake made with wheat flour, which is a very practical and homely symbol in its way. It made its gesture, as the feast that followed did, toward the beginning of a common life. "The cake," Fustel de Coulanges writes, "eaten during the recitation of prayers, in the presence and under the eyes of the domestic divinities, makes the union of husband and wife sacred. Henceforth they are united, man and wife, by the powerful bond of the same worship and the same belief."

I have lingered over this ceremony in such detail because of the three- or four-thousand-year survival of so many of the elements of our own ceremony: the giving of the bride, the procession, the cart (which has been replaced by our limousine), the bride's white dress and veil, the bridal cake, and the custom of carrying the bride across the threshold. And this pattern, growing out of arranged marriages, is very widespread. It is still the basic form of a traditional Chinese wedding, in which the bride also goes by sedan to the husband's house and must not step on the threshold. In some parts of Africa, the girl is accompanied by her female relatives and friends, who sing songs along the way.

Songs and poems about how hard it was for young girls to uproot themselves from their families seem almost universal. We found them among the pygmies of Gabon in equatorial Africa, among Korean girls of the Choson dynasty, in the folk songs of the Polish peasantry, and among the Aztecs. Here, for example, is a lovely song the Gabons sing to a bride:

> Slowly, slowly,
> Child, counting the steps,
> Go away, go away with tears,

With a large heart, with a weary heart,
Without turning your face,
From the house, from the village,
Where your eyes so gaily
Laughed at every corner.

Counting, counting your steps,
Today you go away.
With a large heart, with a weary heart,
Go away, go away below!
Counting, counting your steps,
With a large heart, with a weary heart,
Today you go away.

Keep on your heart
And guard well the flower
Of your mother's garden,
The flower which will say to you:
"I am still loved below!"

Of course, a wedding was also in some sense a girl's coming-of-age ceremony, and there were undoubtedly many young women who were glad to begin their adult lives. There is a charming Polish folk song about a young girl trying to look sorry at leaving home:

The bridegroom comes, she sits on the stove,
Her last, long hour beguiling.
She looks so sad, oh, looks so sad!
In secret she is smiling.

In one mood or another, in most of the cultures of the world, this movement of the young girl from her parental home to the home of her in-laws was the human reality of marriage.

In Greece and Rome, the marriage as a ritual of domestic religion came to be joined with the public religion, and by the time of the epithalamion of Julius Caesar's day the gods and goddesses of fertility, river nymphs and orchard dryads, as well as Zeus and Hera—father sky and mother earth, who never get along very well in the old stories—are also invoked in the wedding songs. These come much closer to the idea of sacred marriage, and the big event in these poems is not a ritual before the family hearth but the consummation in the wedding chamber.

Contemporary anthropologists tend to discuss these marriages as a kind of property exchange and underline the fact that the women were treated as a form of family property used to secure social alliance, an exchange driven by the incest taboo which, in fact, creates the main structural features of a society, its clan relationships. To an older generation of anthropologists these weddings with their procession of the bride looked a lot like a sacrificial ritual, in which the bride's virginity is sacrificed to the spirits of fertility, a letting of blood more or less like the slaying of an animal or human victim. In this sense a wedding is a positive version, because life-giving, of the older form. "Marriage," one student of Hindu culture observes, "not only resembles sacrifice: it supplants sacrifice as an even more efficacious religious event." However one reads it, much of this history lies behind our bridal procession down the aisle to the strains of Mendelssohn's wedding march.

There is also—poets are inveterate readers of symbols—another way to read this moment. Comedy, especially Shakespearean comedy, usually ends with a wedding. The engine of the comedy is sexual desire, or romantic love. To make the sweet blindness of love clear, the plots are usually full of twins, cases of mistaken identity, passionate and wrongheaded fixations, other mishaps. The young people are typically trying to get around their stodgy elders. There's a great deal of confusion, some passage through the blessing of a green world, a Forest of Arden, or the dream forest of *A Midsummer Night's Dream*, or a magical space like Prospero's island in *The Tempest*, and in the end the energy of the young triumphs, in more or less the way every spring overthrows every winter, and the young people get married and the whole social world is fresher and livelier for it. *Romeo and Juliet*, in this way, is a tragedy, because it is a failed comedy. The rivalries and hatreds of the old society are so powerful that the young can't find their way to each other and, instead, they die in each other's arms. This pattern of renewal and failed renewal in the plays suggests that Shakespeare and his society saw a wedding as a sort of folk version of sacred marriage, an overcoming of the old by the new, of winter by spring, and the bride's procession—even with the old ideas of property exchange and ritual sacrifice behind it—as an enactment of the power of the green world itself. As in Botticelli's painting, the bride coming down the aisle is the coming, garlanded with flowers, of spring itself, and a symbol of the endless energy of rebirth. The difference, of course, between this scenario and the one in the old myths of sacred marriage is that the desires of the young, their rebellion and act of free choice, have come into play.

Christianity, when it swept into the pagan world as a form of asceticism, changed the wedding ceremony radically. It was, at the beginning, an end-of-the-world religion, and it was deeply suspicious of sexuality and nature. There was first of all the example of Christ's celibacy, and the myth of his virgin birth and St. Paul's famous ambivalence about marriage. The older feeling for human love survived, borrowed not from Greek myth but from the Hebrew Bible, as Eden, a remembered paradise before the fall, and a wedding was still to be blessed, since it had been created by God. Equally crucial, more crucial perhaps, was that it moved the act of marriage out of the family house and the bridal chamber and onto the altar. With its concern for the human soul, thought of as eternal, it made the vows spoken by two people before the altar of God the center of the sacrament. And, at some early stage, it borrowed from Judaism the ritual of the giving of a ring, in imitation of the patriarchs of old. But the old mythic sense of connection to nature had disappeared.

In Roman Catholic theology, all of the sacraments are ministered by a priest except this one. A marriage is performed by the bride and the groom. They are the ministers of the ceremony, and the priest is only a witness. The marriage is the saying of the vows. The idea is that only by their own free wills can two people marry each other. No one can do it for them, or to them, and this is an enormous shift in the meaning of marriage. Marriages, of course, were still arranged by families. They were still based on male authority and female consent. Much of the sense of sexual joy and of its connection to the powers in nature had been pushed out of the ceremony, but the sense of personal vows made in a public space at once sacred and eternal had been added. And with it one of our own fundamental assumptions about marriage is in place.

Romantic love appeared suddenly in the European Middle Ages in poems and stories like the one about Tristan and Iseult. It was probably first a rebellion against the order of arranged marriages. It was usually adulterous, and it was based on the un-Christian idea of passionate, personal, sexual love. It was, besides being sexual, spiritual and idealizing, and its elaboration was assisted by the Renaissance rediscovery of texts like Plato's *Symposium*, in which all love is a form of yearning for the absolute, a form of the soul's hunger for union with its meaning. Poets charted the stages of passionate love and turned the gestures of courtship into a kind of mystic quest.

All this must have looked like too much fun to be left to adulterers, and so it was gradually assimilated, at least in literature and in the upper classes who read and wrote it, into the ethos of marriage. In the English Renaissance, it also got submitted to some healthy village teasing. You see this in Shakespeare's *A Midsummer Night's Dream*, which is probably the greatest wedding—well, courtship—poem in the English language. At the beginning of the play, Theseus, the Duke of Athens, is awaiting his marriage night. He has four days to go until the full moon, and, looking into the night sky, he speaks the most delicious line of sexual yearning I know: "My hunger lingers me." As soon as he says it, Shakespeare hauls onstage the conflict between arranged marriage and romantic love. An older man appears, to complain to the Duke that his daughter is in love with the wrong young man and won't marry the one he has picked out. He wants permission to kill her if she doesn't do what he says. Theseus instead offers her alternatives: obedient marriage, death, or a nunnery. She chooses the nunnery, but then her lover shows up and they decide to elope—a more practical solution.

The play is drenched in the power and magic and silliness of romantic love. Hymen, the marriage god, presides over it in various guises, but so does Puck, the forest sprite, the spirit of comedy, who thinks that human beings with their hungers and star-struck idealizations are complete nitwits. Still, in the end, Shakespeare gives the lovers to each other and makes the murderous father learn to like it. And in a famous speech at the end of the play, he makes a pact with them, declaring that lovers, lunatics, and poets are made of the same stuff.

So the ancient procession and the sacred vows and the ideal of romantic love were all in place when Europeans began to colonize the American continent. But there was also a deep streak of antifeminism in English culture, as another of Shakespeare's plays, *The Taming of the Shrew*, makes clear. Many of the colonists were, of course, Puritans. And it was the Puritans, contrary to most people's idea of them, who forged the intellectual links between marriage, romantic love, and the idea of personal freedom. They did it, oddly enough, by attacking the Church of England's prohibition of divorce. In the Jewish tradition this issue got argued out by rabbis in the first century B.C.E., but it was, among others, John Milton, the great Puritan poet and author of *Paradise Lost*, who raised it among the English seventeen hundred years later. He wrote a pamphlet making the plausible argument that if people who could not love each other were compelled not to separate and to be faithful to each other, it amounted to treating marriage as stock breeding. If human love was holy, he argued, and if the individual soul mattered, people had to be free to find a mate who shared their heart's affections. This turns out to be one of the deep paradoxes in the history of marriage: that the freedom to marry was established by the freedom to divorce.

This insistence on freedom of choice was, mainly, another attack on arranged marriages, but it put into place another of our assumptions about marriage, that it is a vow made freely out of love. Divorce was still very much disapproved of, and the Puritan model, if anything, intensified the idea of the family run by a male patriarch, but the conception of marriage which the Puritans brought to America assumed, at least in theory, that it was a union made freely by two people who loved each other. And it assumed that the sexual love between them—as you will see in Milton's treatment of Adam and Eve in the garden, which we have included among the selections of poetry—was a very good thing.

Still, at the time of this country's founding, the situation was, in England and America, and in most of the rest of the world, that women were legally disenfranchised by marriage. Much of the poetry about marriage written by women in the last three centuries, while the battles went on to give them a legal standing in their marriages, was skeptical or ironic, though in the nineteenth century there also developed a lot of that Victorian sentimentality about the angel at the hearth that still clings to most of the literature of weddings in bookstores today. Emily Dickinson, an heir to the American Puritan tradition, lived when the sentimental tradition was at full flood, and she rejected it. She was an exceedingly brave and adventurous spirit. She wrote passionate and amazing love poems, and seems to have thought of personal love as its own sacrament—

> The Sweetest Heresy received
> That Man and Woman know—
> Each Other's Convert—
> Though the Faith accommodate but Two—

but was frankly dubious about the official institution:

> "My husband"—women say—
> Stroking the melody—
> Is *this*—the way?

Much of modern literature has done the work of leeching the poisons from the tensions created by—among other things—the idealizations and the unfairness in the relationship. Other poets, Dickinson among them, and D. H. Lawrence and Rainer Maria Rilke, were exploring the meaning of an intense, enduring, intimate relation with another person, and the human hunger it is born of. That work continues, just as the legal and political struggle to establish marriage and other relationships on a basis of equality has now mostly been won. Our ceremonies usually assume this, though not always, as my friends in Atlanta found out.

As we read through this history and talked to friends, Stephen Mitchell and I began to get a better sense of why people were looking for poems to be read at their weddings. First of all, it seems that the Christian conception of marriage, while it established the personal vows, tended to push away the deep connection of marriage to the natural cosmos and to what is magical to us in the processes of nature, and people want that brought back in. Second, they want, besides an elaboration of the duties of marriage, a more intense expression of the meaning of personal love and a deeper sense of marriage as a personal and spiritual path set out on by the two partners. And, finally, they want inside the sacred ceremony a deeper sense of joy and of play. We have offered a lot of the best work from inside our own traditions for this purpose, and also from outside it, from older cultures and other spiritual traditions.

It is our hope that couples who think about the symbolic meanings in their wedding ceremony and use some of the poems to complement the words of the ceremony will be able to shape a wedding that says what they want it to say. There is much to gather: the old sense of divine and cosmic marriage as a right relation of sexuality to the earth, the sense of the comedy and delight of anarchic human energy, of the making of a new world and a new pattern of family relations, the sacred vows that require steadfastness and commitment and are made in a space both holy and in some way eternal, the expression of those vows in the sweetness of personal sexual love and their duration in the comfort of companionship, of the shared parenting of children, in the rhythm of days, in the intensities and difficulties of knowing and being known by another person with whom a life is shared on the condition of equality.

It may not be easy to find the ways to either say these things or enact them, and the project may seem hopelessly ideal, but they are what ceremony was invented for. The Irish poet William Butler Yeats put it this way on the occasion of his daughter's marriage:

> How but in custom and in ceremony
> Are innocence and beauty born?

I began with an image of the dream-wish at the heart of many weddings. Here, finally, is an image of marriage. This is also drawn from literature, perhaps the oldest poem in the European tradition. In the *Odyssey*, one of the Greek heroes, Menelaos, is trying to get back home after ten years of war. The poem is about the wanderings of Odysseus around a mostly mythical and strange Mediterranean Sea, during which he encounters a giant one-eyed cannibal, monsters, various temptresses and sorceresses who keep putting him off his goal. Menelaos's adventure is a variation on the theme. A goddess reveals to him that the only one who can tell him the way home is a strange sea-god named Proteus, which in Greek means something like "first person" and has come in English to mean "ceaseless change." When Menelaos sees Proteus in the water, he is told, he has to dive in, grab hold, and wrestle out of him the way home. Proteus has the ability to assume every possible shape, imaginable and unimaginable. He can take the form of every terror, every delight. Menelaos is going to seem to himself to be wrestling with monsters, with fear, rage, self-disgust, shame, depression, boredom, exhaustion, all of which will make him long to let go. He is going to wrestle with magical creatures of great beauty, lightheartedness, laughter, rapture, contentment, ecstasy, joy, all of which may tempt him to relax his determination and let go. But if he does not let go, he will be able to return to his kingdom, to his orchards and vineyards, and to his marriage bed. This has always seemed to me an image of the task of marriage over time. Proteus is, of course, not so much the other person, but ourselves. The task is to understand that and to hold on, which means, I think, to cultivate that quality of presence I spoke of at the beginning of this essay, and with it to extort from the sea-god that blessing that sends us home.

The poems follow—"and the rest of the song," as Catullus says in his wedding poem, "is your singing."

ROBERT HASS

A Note on the selections:
We found ourselves excerpting from longer poems and editing them, so that the best parts might make readings of an appropriate length. We also found with some of the older poems that we wanted their music in this book, but not necessarily all of their sentiments. So we made adaptations. There are places where a blushing bride who stood at the altar in the sixteenth century has been replaced by a young

couple. Some people may feel that it is a desecration to rewrite old poems, but in fact the old poets did it all the time, and the poems themselves are easy to get hold of and will survive whatever we've done with them. As Chaucer's Wife of Bath said in another context, if you light your candle on someone else's, theirs still gives light.

R. H.

READINGS

from *Love Song*

Everything that touches us, me and you,
takes us together like a violin's bow,
which draws *one* voice out of two separate strings.
Upon what instrument are we two spanned?
And what musician holds us in his hand?
Oh sweetest song.

RAINER MARIA RILKE
translated by Stephen Mitchell

The Two of You

Don't run anymore. Quiet. How softly it rains
On the roofs of the city. How perfect
All things are. Now, for the two of you
Waking up in a royal bed by a garret window.
For a man and a woman. For one plant divided
Into masculine and feminine which longed for each other.
Yes, this is my gift to you. Above ashes
On a bitter, bitter earth. Above the subterranean
Echo of clamorings and vows. So that now at dawn
You must be attentive: the tilt of a head,
A hand with a comb, two faces in a mirror
Are only forever once, even if unremembered,
So that you watch what is, though it fades away,
And are grateful every moment for your being.
Let that little park with greenish marble busts
In the pearl-gray light, under a summer drizzle,
Remain as it was when you opened the gate.
And the street of tall peeling porticoes
Which this love of yours suddenly transformed.

CZESLAW MILOSZ
translated by the author and Robert Hass

*W*ild Nights—Wild Nights!
Were I with thee
Wild Nights should be
Our luxury!

Futile—the Winds—
To a Heart in port—
Done with the Compass—
Done with the Chart!

Rowing in Eden—
Ah, the Sea!
Might I but moor—Tonight—
In Thee!

EMILY DICKINSON

Of all the Souls that stand create—
I have elected—One—
When Sense from Spirit—files away—
And Subterfuge—is done—
When that which is—and that which was—
Apart—intrinsic—stand—
And this brief Drama in the flesh—
Is shifted—like a Sand—
When Figures show their royal Front—
And Mists—are carved away,
Behold the Atom—I preferred—
To all the lists of Clay!

EMILY DICKINSON

At the Wedding March

God with honour hang your head,
Groom, and grace you, bride, your bed
With lissome scions, sweet scions,
Out of hallowed bodies bred.

Each be other's comfort kind:
Déep, déeper than divined,
Divine charity, dear charity,
Fast you ever, fast bind.

Then let the March tread our ears:
I to him turn with tears
Who to wedlock, his wonder wedlock,
Déals tríumph and immortal years.

GERARD MANLEY HOPKINS

*"Scion" means, literally, "twig, offshoot." In reading the poem aloud, you might
want to change this line to: "with lissome daughters, sweet sons." Or if children
aren't a concern: "with lissome beauty, sweet joy."*

Song

Do not fear to put thy feet
Naked in the river sweet;
Think not leech, or newt, or toad
Will bite thy foot, when thou hast trod:
Nor let the water rising high
As thou wad'st in, make thee cry
And sob; but ever live with me
And not a wave shall trouble thee.

JOHN FLETCHER

*N*ow you will feel no rain,
for each of you will be a shelter to the other.

Now you will feel no cold,
for each of you will be warmth to the other.

Now there is no loneliness for you;
now there is no more loneliness.

Now you are two bodies,
but there is only one life before you.

Go now to your dwelling place,
to enter into your days together.

And may your days be good
and long on the earth.

APACHE SONG
translator unknown

Sonnet XVII

I don't love you as if you were the salt-rose, topaz
or arrow of carnations that propagate fire:
I love you as certain dark things are loved,
secretly, between the shadow and the soul.

I love you as the plant that doesn't bloom and carries
hidden within itself the light of those flowers,
and thanks to your love, darkly in my body
lives the dense fragrance that rises from the earth.

I love you without knowing how, or when, or from where,
I love you simply, without problems or pride:
I love you in this way because I don't know any other way of loving

but this, in which there is no I or you,
so intimate that your hand upon my chest is my hand,
so intimate that when I fall asleep it is your eyes that close.

PABLO NERUDA
translated by Stephen Mitchell

You that love Lovers,
this is your home. Welcome!

In the midst of making form, Love
made this form that melts form,
with love for the door, and
Soul, the vestibule.

Watch the dust grains moving
in the light near the window.

Their dance is our dance.

We rarely hear the inward music,
but we're all dancing to it nevertheless,

directed by what teaches us,
the pure joy of the sun,
our Music Master.

RUMI
translated by Coleman Barks with A. J. Arberry

*Jelaluddin Rumi (1207–1273) was a Sufi mystic and founder of the Mevlevi, the
ecstatic dancing order known in the West as the Whirling Dervishes. In 1244 he
met the wandering dervish Shams al-Din ("the Sun of Religion") of Tabriz: an
overwhelming experience which led Rumi into the depths of divine love. "With
Shams," Coleman Barks writes, "he discovered the inner Friend, the soul, the
Beloved, a constant reminder of God's presence. However one might try to name
that mystery, out of its love, joy, and longing came the poetry, the enormous* Divani
Shamsi Tabriz *(42,000 lines) and the six-volume* Mathnawi. *Rumi did not see
the separate streams of different religions, but rather the ocean into which they were
pouring. 'I go into the Christian church,' he said, 'and the Jewish synagogue, and
the Muslim mosque, and I see* one *altar.'"*

I'll give my love an apple without a core,
I'll give my love a house without a door,
I'll give my love a palace wherein she may be,
And she may unlock it without any key.

My head is the apple without a core,
My mind is the house without a door,
My heart is the palace wherein she may be,
And she may unlock it without any key.

ANONYMOUS

This can be spoken by or for the bride, the groom, or both, with simple changes of pronoun.

Married Love

You and I
Have so much love
That it
Burns like a fire,
In which we bake a lump of clay
Molded into a figure of you
And a figure of me.
Then we take both of them,
And break them into pieces,
And mix the pieces with water,
And mold again a figure of you,
And a figure of me.
I am in your clay.
You are in my clay.
In life we share a single quilt.
In death we will share one bed.

KUAN TAO-SHENG
translated by Kenneth Rexroth and Ling Chung

"*Kuan Tao-sheng (1262–1319), was famous not only as a poet," Ling Chung writes,
"but also as a calligrapher and painter. She was the wife of Chao Meng-fu, one of
the most famous calligraphers and painters in Chinese history.*"

We Two, How Long We Were Fool'd

We two, how long we were fool'd,
Now transmuted, we swiftly escape as Nature escapes,
We are Nature, long have we been absent, but now we return,
We become plants, trunks, foliage, roots, bark,
We are bedded in the ground, we are rocks,
We are oaks, we grow in the openings side by side,
We browse, we are two among the wild herds spontaneous as any,
We are two fishes swimming in the sea together,
We are what locust blossoms are, we drop scent around lanes mornings
    and evenings,
We are also the coarse smut of beasts, vegetables, minerals,
We are two predatory hawks, we soar above and look down,
We are two resplendent suns, we it is who balance ourselves orbic and
    stellar, we are as two comets,
We prowl fang'd and four-footed in the woods, we spring on prey,
We are two clouds forenoons and afternoons driving overhead,
We are seas mingling, we are two of those cheerful waves rolling over
    each other and interwetting each other,
We are what the atmosphere is, transparent, receptive, pervious,
    impervious,
We are snow, rain, cold, darkness, we are each product and influence of
    the globe,
We have circled and circled till we have arrived home again, we two,
We have voided all but freedom and all but our own joy.

WALT WHITMAN

A Wedding Toast

St. John tells how, at Cana's wedding-feast,
The water-pots poured wine in such amount
That by his sober count
There were a hundred gallons at the least.

It made no earthly sense, unless to show
How whatsoever love elects to bless
Brims to a sweet excess
That can without depletion overflow.

Which is to say that what love sees is true;
That the world's fullness is not made but found.
Life hungers to abound
And pour its plenty out for such as you.

Now, if your loves will lend an ear to mine,
I toast you both, good son and dear new daughter.
May you not lack for water,
And may that water smack of Cana's wine.

RICHARD WILBUR

from *The Imitation of Christ*

Love is a great thing, a great good in every way; it alone lightens what is heavy, and leads smoothly over all roughness. For it carries a burden without being burdened, and makes every bitter thing sweet and tasty. Love wants to be lifted up, not held back by anything low. Love wants to be free, and far from all worldly desires, so that its inner vision may not be dimmed and good fortune bind it or misfortune cast it down. Nothing is sweeter than love; nothing stronger, nothing higher, nothing wider; nothing happier, nothing fuller, nothing better in heaven and earth; for love is born of God . . .

Love keeps watch and is never unaware, even when it sleeps; tired, it is never exhausted; hindered, it is never defeated; alarmed, it is never afraid; but like a living flame and a burning torch it bursts upward and blazes forth . . . .

Love is quick, sincere, dutiful, joyous, and pleasant; brave, patient, faithful, prudent, serene, and vigorous; and it never seeks itself. For whenever we seek ourselves, we fall away from love. Love is watchful, humble, and upright; not weak, or frivolous, or directed toward vain things; temperate, pure, steady, calm, and alert in all the senses. Love is devoted and thankful to God, always trusting and hoping in him, even when it doesn't taste his sweetness, for without pain no one can live in love.

THOMAS À KEMPIS
translated by Stephen Mitchell

This has been excerpted from a longer passage; see pages 141–142. In describing the devout Christian's love of God, it also describes the love of a devoted husband or wife.

*I*s it for now or for always,
The world hangs on a stalk?
Is it a trick or a trysting place,
The woods we have found to walk?

Is it a mirage or a miracle,
Your lips that lift at mine:
And the suns like a juggler's juggling-balls,
Are they a sham or a sign?

Shine out, my sudden angel,
Break fear with breast and brow,
I take you now and for always,
For always is always now.

PHILIP LARKIN

The Owl and the Pussy-Cat

The Owl and the Pussy-Cat went to sea
    In a beautiful pea-green boat:
They took some honey, and plenty of money
    Wrapped up in a five-pound note.
The Owl looked up to the stars above,
    And sang to a small guitar,
"O lovely Pussy, O Pussy, my love,
    What a beautiful Pussy you are,
        You are,
        You are!
    What a beautiful Pussy you are!"

Pussy said to the Owl, "You elegant fowl,
    How charmingly sweet you sing!
Oh! let us be married; too long we have tarried:
    But what shall we do for a ring?"
They sailed away, for a year and a day,
    To the land where the bong-tree grows;
And there in a wood a Piggy-wig stood,
    With a ring at the end of his nose,
        His nose,
        His nose,
    With a ring at the end of his nose.

"Dear Pig, are you willing to sell for one shilling
    Your ring?" Said the Piggy, "I will."
So they took it away, and were married next day
    By the Turkey who lives on the hill.
They dined on mince and slices of quince,
    Which they ate with a runcible spoon;
And hand in hand, on the edge of the sand,
    They danced by the light of the moon,

The moon,
The moon,
They danced by the light of the moon.

EDWARD LEAR

It might be most fun if this poem is read by members of the wedding party together or in alternating stanzas.

Psalm 1

Blessed are the man and the woman
    who have grown beyond themselves
    and have seen through their separations.
They delight in the way things are
    and keep their hearts open, day and night.
They are like trees planted near flowing rivers,
    which bear fruit when they are ready.
Their leaves will not fall or wither.
    Everything they do will succeed.

THE BOOK OF PSALMS
adapted by Stephen Mitchell

from *Letters to a Young Poet*

For one human being to love another human being: that is perhaps the most difficult task that has been entrusted to us, the ultimate task, the final test and proof, the work for which all other work is merely preparation. Loving does not at first mean merging, surrendering, and uniting with another person—it is a high inducement for the individual to ripen, to become something in himself, to become world, to become world in himself for the sake of another person; it is a great, demanding claim on him, something that chooses him and calls him to vast distances.

RAINER MARIA RILKE
translated by Stephen Mitchell

The passages on this and the next page have been excerpted from a longer statement on love; see pages 151–153. These deeply moving and often prophetic letters were written in 1904 by the poet whom many consider to be the greatest of the twentieth century.

from *Letters to a Young Poet*

Someday there will be girls and women whose name will no longer mean the mere opposite of the male, but something in itself, something that makes one think not of any complement, but only of life and reality: the female human being.

This advance will transform the love experience, which is now filled with error, will change it from the ground up, and reshape it into a relationship that is meant to be between one human being and another, no longer one that flows from man to woman. And this more human love (which will fulfill itself with infinite consideration and gentleness, and kindness and clarity in binding and releasing) will resemble what we are now preparing painfully and with great struggle: the love that consists in this: that two solitudes protect and border and greet each other.

RAINER MARIA RILKE
translated by Stephen Mitchell

The first sentence in this selection, because it was written so long ago, may need revising when it is read aloud. You can say, "Now there are girls and women . . ." and change the tenses throughout.

The final sentence conveys a truth that Rilke felt deeply. In "Requiem for a Friend" he said it this way:

We need, in love, to practice only this:
letting each other go. For holding on
comes easily; we do not need to learn it.

from *Letters*

Once the realization is accepted that even between the closest people
infinite distances exist, a marvelous living side-by-side can grow up for
them, if they succeed in loving the expanse between them, which gives
them the possibility of always seeing each other as a whole and before an
immense sky.

RAINER MARIA RILKE
translated by Stephen Mitchell

*This statement of Rilke's may be the most powerful in the book. See the complete
passage on pages 154–155.*

from *A Wedding*

Into the enormous sky flew
a whirlwind of blue-gray patches—
a flock of doves spiraling up
suddenly from the dovecotes.

And to see them makes you wish,
just as the wedding-feast is ending,
years of happiness for this couple,
flung onto the wind like doves.

Life too is only an instant,
only a dissolving of ourselves
into everyone,
as if we gave ourselves as gifts.

Only a wedding, only the depths
of a window and the sound rushing in,
only a song, or a dream,
only a blue-gray dove.

BORIS PASTERNAK
adapted by Robert Hass and Stephen Mitchell

Come, my beloved, let us go up the shining mountain, and sit together;
  we will watch the sun go down in beauty from that shining place.
We will sit there till the Night Traveler rises in beauty above the shining
  mountain; we will watch him as he climbs to the skies.
We will watch also the little stars following their chief.
We will watch the northern lights playing their game of ball in their
  cold, glistening country.
We will sit there on the beautiful mountain while the thunder beats his
  drum.
We will see the flashes from the lit pipe of the lightning.
We will see the great whirlwind race with the squall.
We will sit there until all creatures drowse.
There we will hear the great owl sing his usual song: "Go to sleep, go to
  sleep," and see all animals obey his call.
We will sit there in beauty on the mountain, and watch the small stars
  in their sleepless flight.
They do not mind the song "Go to sleep"; we will not mind it either,
  but sit more closely together, and think of nothing but ourselves,
  on the beautiful mountain.
Again it will be heard: "Go to sleep, go to sleep," and the Night
  Traveler will come closer, to warn us that everything is sleeping
  except ourselves and the little stars.
They and their chief are coursing along, and our minds go with them.
Then the owl sleeps; and his call to sleep sleeps; and the lightnings flash
  from a long way off; the great pipe is going out; and the thunder
  ceases to beat his drum; and though our bodies urge us to sleep,
  we sit in beauty, very still, upon the shining mountain.

ABANAKI SONG
from the translation of John Reade
(adapted by Robert Hass)

*T*he tongues of the lightning Snakes flicker and twist, one to the other.
They flash across the foliage of the cabbage palms.
Lightning flashes through the clouds with the flickering tongues of the
      snakes.
It is always there, at the wide expanse of water, at the place of the
      sacred tree.
All over the sky their tongues flicker, above the place called Rising
      Clouds, the place called Standing Clouds.
All over the sky tongues flickering and twisting.
They are always there at the camp by the wide expanse of water.
All over the sky the tongues flicker: at the place called Two Sisters
      where the guardian ancestors are
Lightning flashes through the clouds, flash of the Lightning Snake.
Its blinding flash lights up the cabbage palms,
Gleams on the cabbage palms and on the shining leaves.

ABORIGINAL AUSTRALIAN SONG
from the translation of R. M. and C. H. Berndt
(adapted by Robert Hass)

C. M. Bowra in his Primitive Song *provides a gloss on this song: "Spirits are at*
work in the courting-season, and in north-eastern Arnhem Land the aboriginals
associate love with the season of the monsoons, when the flashes of lightning in the
sky are identified with snakes, which are a symbol of mating among many peoples.
Here lovemaking is associated with supernatural and natural powers and partakes
of their strength and magnificence."

"Lavender's blue, dilly, dilly, lavender's green,
  When I am King, dilly, dilly, you shall be Queen."
"Who told you so, dilly, dilly, who told you so?"
" 'Twas mine own heart, dilly, dilly, that told me so.

"Call up your men, dilly, dilly, set them to work,
  Some with a rake, dilly, dilly, some with a fork,
  Some to make hay, dilly, dilly, some to thresh corn,
  While you and I, dilly, dilly, keep ourselves warm."

"If it should hap, dilly, dilly, if it should chance,
  We shall be gay, dilly, dilly, we shall both dance.
  Lavender's blue, dilly, dilly, lavender's green,
  You shall be King, dilly, dilly, when I am Queen."

ANONYMOUS

Sukey, you shall be my wife
And I will tell you why:
I have got a little pig,
And you have got a sty;
I have got a dun cow,
And you can make good cheese.
Sukey, will you marry me?
Say Yes, if you please.

ANONYMOUS

The Peace: A Wedding Song

It's time to say words of good omen
And to bring forth the bridegroom and the bride.
It's time for us to take torches and dance and rejoice.
We can take the farm tools back to the fields
After we've danced and poured wine and chased out bad luck
And after we've prayed to the gods of earth, sea, and sky
To help us to an ample life,
To grant us a good crop of barley
And plenty of wine
And figs to munch on,
And that we bring forth children, supple-limbed, loud at their play,
And that all the good things we lose by war
Are returned to us when we gather ripe fruit for the wedding feast
And the fiery sword has been put away.

ARISTOPHANES
adapted by Robert Hass

Variation on the Word Sleep

I would like to watch you sleeping.
I would like to watch you,
sleeping. I would like to sleep
with you, to enter
your sleep as its smooth dark wave
slides over my head

and walk with you through that lucent
wavering forest of bluegreen leaves
with its watery sun & three moons
towards the cave where you must descend,
towards your worst fear

I would like to give you the silver
branch, the small white flower, the one
word that will protect you
from the grief at the center
of your dream, from the grief
at the center. I would like to follow
you up the long stairway
again & become
the boat that would row you back
carefully, a flame
in two cupped hands
to where your body lies
beside me, and you enter
it as easily as breathing in

I would like to be the air
that inhabits you for a moment

only. I would like to be that unnoticed
& that necessary.

MARGARET ATWOOD

Shoshone Wedding Song

Him:
"Not a spirit, not a bird,
  That was my flute you heard
  Last night by the river.
  When you came with your wicker jar
  Where the river tugs at the willows,
  That was my flute you heard
  Calling, Come to the willows."

Her:
"Not a spirit, not a bird
  Made the lupine rustle.
  That was my heart you heard
  And the rustle of my hem
  As I walked in the grasses.
  That was my heart you heard
  When you came to the willows."

MARY AUSTIN
adapted by Robert Hass

The Dance

I would have each couple turn,
join and unjoin, be lost
in the greater turning
of other couples, woven
in the circle of a dance,
the song of long time flowing

over them, so they may return,
turn again in to themselves
out of desire greater than their own,
belonging to all, to each,
to the dance, and to the song
that moves them through the night.

What is fidelity? To what
does it hold? The point
of departure, or the turning road
that is departure and absence
and the way home? What we are
and what we were once

are far estranged. For those
who would not change, time
is infidelity. But we are married
until death, and are betrothed
to change. By silence, so,
I learn my song. I earn

my sunny fields by absence, once
and to come. And I love you

as I love the dance that brings you
out of the multitude
in which you come and go.
Love changes, and in change is true.

WENDELL BERRY

from *Several Questions Answered*

What is it men in women do require?
The lineaments of Gratified Desire.
What is it women do in men require?
The lineaments of Gratified Desire.

WILLIAM BLAKE

In the Month of May

In the month of May when all leaves open,
I see when I walk how well all things
lean on each other, how the bees work,
the fish make their living the first day.
Monarchs fly high; then I understand
I love you with what in me is unfinished.

I love you with what in me is still
changing, what has no head or arms
or legs, what has not found its body.
And why shouldn't the miraculous,
caught on this earth, visit
the old man alone in his hut?

And why shouldn't Gabriel, who loves honey,
be fed with our own radishes and walnuts?
And lovers, tough ones, how many there are
whose holy bodies are not yet born.
Along the roads, I see so many places
I would like us to spend the night.

ROBERT BLY

Psalm 100

Sing to the Lord, all creatures!
    Worship him with your joy;
    praise him with the sound of your laughter.
Know that we all belong to him,
    that he is our source and our home.
Enter his light with thanksgiving;
    fill your hearts with his praise.
For his goodness is beyond comprehension,
    and his deep love endures forever.

THE BOOK OF PSALMS
adapted by Stephen Mitchell

This and the following psalm weren't originally wedding songs. But they are moments of pure celebration.

God—the ultimate, radiant, unnamable reality that is the source and essence of all things—is not, of course, a he or a she; but because English has no personal pronoun to express what transcends gender, we have to call God him or her. Lao-tzu, wonderfully, calls "him" "it":

There was something formless and perfect
before the universe was born.
It is serene. Empty.
Solitary. Unchanging.
Infinite. Eternally present.
It is the mother of the universe.
For lack of a better name,
I call it the Tao.

s. m.

Psalm 148

Praise God in the highest heavens;
    praise him beyond the stars.
Praise him, you bodhisattvas,
    and you angels burning with his love.
Praise him in the depths of matter,
    praise him in atomic space.
Praise him, you whirling electrons,
    you unimaginable quarks.
Praise him in lifeless galaxies;
    praise him from the pit of black holes.
Praise him, creatures on all planets,
    inconceivable forms of life.
Let them all praise the Unnamable,
    for he is their source, their home.
He made them in all their beauty
    and the laws by which they exist.

Praise God upon the earth,
    whales and all creatures of the sea,
fire, hail, snow, and frost,
    hurricanes fulfilling his command,
mountains and barren hills,
    fruit trees and cedar forests,
wild animals and tame,
    reptiles, insects, birds,
creatures invisible to the eye,
    and tiniest one-celled beings,
rich and poor, powerful
    and oppressed, dark-skinned and light-skinned,
men and women alike,
    old and young together.
Let them praise the Unnamable God,

whose goodness is the breath of life,
who has made us in his own image,
    the light that fills heaven and earth.

THE BOOK OF PSALMS
adapted by Stephen Mitchell

"All night the cicada chirps;
all day the grasshopper jumps.
Before I saw my love,
my heart was confused.
But now that I have seen him,
now that I have met him,
my heart is calm."

"I climbed the southern hill
to pick the fern shoots.
Before I saw my love,
my heart was troubled.
But now that I have seen her,
now that I have met her,
my heart is at peace.

"I climbed the southern hill
to pick the bracken shoots.
Before I saw my love,
my heart was sad.
But now that I have seen her,
now that I have met her,
my heart is serene."

THE BOOK OF SONGS
adapted from the translation of Arthur Waley

*The Book of Songs, an anthology reportedly compiled by Confucius, contains the
oldest folksongs in the Chinese tradition. Some of them may date from as early as
1000 B.C.E.*

Unlimited Friendliness

This is what should be done by the man and woman who are wise, who seek the good, and who know the meaning of the place of peace.

Let them be fervent, upright, and sincere, without conceit of self, easily contented and joyous, free of cares; let them not be submerged by the things of the world; let them not take upon themselves the burden of worldly goods; let their senses be controlled; let them be wise but not puffed up, and let them not desire great possessions even for their families. Let them do nothing that is mean or that the wise would reprove.

May all beings be happy and at their ease. May they be joyous and live in safety.

All beings, whether weak or strong—omitting none—in high, middle, or low realms of existence, small or great, visible or invisible, near or far away, born or to be born: may all beings be happy and at their ease.

Let none deceive another, or despise any being in any state. Let none by anger or ill-will wish harm to another.

Even as a mother watches over and protects her only child, so with a boundless mind should one cherish all living beings, radiating friendliness over the entire world, above, below, and all around without limit. So let them cultivate a boundless good will toward the entire world, unlimited, free from ill-will or enmity.

Standing or walking, sitting or lying down, during all their waking hours, let them establish this mindfulness of good will, which is the highest state.

Abandoning vain discussions, having a clear vision, free from sense appetites, those who are perfect will never again know rebirth.

THE BUDDHA
translated by Edward Conze

This great teaching, though not explicitly about marriage, has been used at many American Buddhist wedding ceremonies. It points us toward our true nature, which manifests itself as a serene and effortless generosity.
    S. M.

O, my luve's like a red, red rose   love's
    That's newly sprung in June;
O, my luve's like the melodie
    That's sweetly played in tune.

As fair thou art, my bonnie lass,
    So deep in luve am I;
And I will luve thee still, my dear,
    Till a' the seas gang dry.   all; go

Till a' the seas gang dry, my dear,
    And the rocks melt wi' the sun;
I will luve thee still, my dear,
    While the sands o' life shall run.

ROBERT BURNS

Roman Epithalamion

Dweller on Helicon, son
of the muse of the stars' slow
turning through the night sky, god
who hastens the tender bride
to her bridegroom, we sing your name:
    O Hymen Hymenaee, Hymenaee.

Cover your head with a garland
of fragrant red marjoram flowers,
put on your flame-colored mantle,
come happily, wearing yellow
      slippers on your snowy feet!

Waking on this festive morning,
chanting the poems of marriage
in a sweetly tremulant voice,
pound the earth under your feet,
      whirl the pine torch in your hand,

for today _____ marries
_____ , who is as lovely
as Venus was at Idalia
when Paris chose her among the goddesses;
      they go with good auspices,

as dear as the Asian myrtle is
to the nymphs of the forest
who love their flowery playthings,
brilliant with sprigs of white blossoms,
      and feed them on dewdrops.

Come to us quickly, marriage-god.
Set about leaving your shelter,
your cave on the mountain cooled
by clear water from the stream
    of the nymph Aganippe.

Call to their home these new lovers,
eager to be with each other,
fasten their hearts with affection
as trailing ivy will fasten close
    around the trunk of an oak.

And you too, young men and women,
for whom a day just like this one
approaches, cry out in measure,
sing out the god's name: *O Hymen*
    Hymenaee, Hymenaee,

so he will come all the faster,
summoned by your songs
to his duties, this herald
of the Venus of days, this god who
    seals passionate desire.

What god more lovingly called on
by those whose love is requited?
Whom shall men worship more in all
heaven? *O Hymen Hymenaee,*
    Hymen Hymenaee.

Worried fathers invoke you;
for your sake, young girls loosen
the bindings that gather their dresses;
the nervous young bridegrooms
    jump at the sound of your music!

You give the budding girl over
to the hands of her husband,
you give the boy to his wife,
and pluck them both from their mother's
bosoms. *O Hymen Hymenaee,*
Hymen Hymenaee.

Without you Venus is for hours,
she is not the one of long years,
of excellent accomplishment, yet
when you are willing, she abides.
What god compares to this one?

No house may have heirs without you
nor aged parents have children
to lean on; yet they may have them
and more, when you are willing.
What god compares to this one?

A land that gave you no worship
would not have young to tend it, to honor
the earth against her despoilers.
When you are willing, we have them.
What god compares to this one?

Roman tradition calls now for a few
bawdy verses. We're not implying
that in the case of you two
it would be in any way appropriate.
O Hymen Hymenaee.

But it sometimes happens that the young
have their flings, catastrophic passions,
those relationships that practically kill you,
that you tell yourself you learned from.
  O Hymen Hymenaee.

In old Rome a couple of pretty kids
used to toss walnuts to the crowd
for the bride and the bridegroom.
I think the nuts must have symbolized
    old boyfriends and girlfriends.

We're not saying you two went cruising,
picked people up on vacation, but
throw out some walnuts anyway;
that frantic life, even if it was
kind of fun, is done with.
  O Hymen Hymenaee.

But now we're finished delaying;
here you are at the altar.
May Venus assist you, since it's plain
that you wish what you wish for,
    this love with its freshness.

Anyone who wants to count the thousands
of joys before you, the days of delight,
may tally the glittering stars
or go counting sands in the desert.
  O Hymen Hymenaee.

Play as you're pleased to. Be children
together and grownups. And show us
some children eventually, as alive
as you two are on this festive day
    and at least as good-looking.

So, god of marriage, we've brought them
this far, and the rest of the song
is their singing. Be good to each other,
you two, and get to work on the singing,
    on the labor of loving.

O Hymen, Hymanaee, Hymenaee.

CATULLUS
from the translation of Charles Martin
(adapted by Robert Hass)

Catullus is one of the great lyric poets of classical Rome. This epithalamion, dating
from about 50 B.C.E., is supposed to be modeled on one by Sappho. It is probably the
oldest surviving complete epithalamion in classical literature. This is an imitation of
it, not a literal translation. It may be too long for anyone to want to read the whole
thing at their wedding, but it can be excerpted.
    R. H.

Epithalamion

Long may this happy heaven-tied band
    Exercise its most holy art,
Keeping her heart within his hand,
     Keeping his hand upon her heart;
       Except from her eyes
         Feel he no charms;
       Find she no joy
         But in his arms;
May each maintain a well-fledged nest
Of winged loves in either's breast;
Be each of them a mutual sacrifice
       Of either's eyes.

May their whole life a sweet song prove
    Set to two well-composed parts
By music's noblest master, Love,
     Played on the strings of both their hearts;
       Whose mutual sound
         May ever meet
       In a just round
         Not short though sweet;
Long may heaven listen to the song

And think it short though it be long;
Oh, prove't a well-set song indeed, which shows
      Sweetest in the close.

RICHARD CRASHAW
adapted by Robert Hass

*Richard Crashaw was a Roman Catholic poet from the great age of Bach and
Roman fountains, the Baroque, which is probably why he likens marriage to a
song. It's the exquisite harmonies of the seventeenth century that he probably has
in mind. The music of the poem is quite wonderful and will need rehearsing.*
    *If the last lines of the first stanza seem a little weird, it's because they are.
Crashaw liked to entertain farfetched ideas. In this case he is playing with the
notion that love is blind. These lovers, blind to anything but each other, are sac-
rificing their roving eyes on the altar of love. (The bride and bridegroom may
want to think through their notions of the extent of specular fidelity before
going with this one, despite its sweet rhymes.)*
    R. H.

*i*f everything happens that can't be done
(and anything's righter
than books
could plan)
the stupidest teacher will almost guess
(with a run
skip
around we go yes)
there's nothing as something as one

one hasn't a why or because or although
(and buds know better
than books
don't grow)
one's anything old being everything new
(with a what
which
around we come who)
one's everyanything so

so world is a leaf so tree is a bough
(and birds sing sweeter
than books
tell how)
so here is away and so your is a my
(with a down
up
around again fly)
forever was never till now

now i love you and you love me
(and books are shuter
than books
can be)
and deep in the high that does nothing but fall

(with a shout
each
around we go all)
there's somebody calling who's we

we're anything brighter than even the sun
(we're everything greater
than books
might mean)
we're everyanything more than believe
(with a spin
leap
alive we're alive)
we're wonderful one times one

E. E. CUMMINGS

*l*ove is more thicker than forget
more thinner than recall
more seldom than a wave is wet
more frequent than to fail

it is most mad and moonly
and less it shall unbe
than all the sea which only
is deeper than the sea

love is less always than to win
less never than alive
less bigger than the least begin
less littler than forgive

it is most sane and sunly
and more it cannot die
than all the sky which only
is higher than the sky

E. E. CUMMINGS

from *The Divine Comedy*

"The love of God, unutterable and perfect,
      flows into a pure soul the way that light
      rushes into a transparent object.
The more love that it finds, the more it gives
      itself; so that, as we grow clear and open,
      the more complete the joy of loving is.
And the more souls who resonate together,
      the greater the intensity of their love,
      for, mirror-like, each soul reflects the others."

DANTE
translated by Stephen Mitchell

It was a quiet way—
He asked if I was his—
I made no answer of the Tongue
But answer of the Eyes—
And then He bore me on
Before this mortal noise
With swiftness, as of Chariots
And distance, as of Wheels.
This World did drop away
As Acres from the feet
Of one that leaneth from Balloon
Upon an Ether street.
The Gulf behind was not,
The Continents were new—
Eternity it was before
Eternity was due.
No Seasons were to us—
It was not Night nor Morn—
But Sunrise stopped upon the place
And fastened it in Dawn.

EMILY DICKINSON

I gave myself to Him—
And took Himself, for Pay,
The solemn contract of a Life
Was ratified, this way—

The Wealth might disappoint—
Myself a poorer prove
Than this great Purchaser suspect,
The Daily Own—of Love

Depreciate the Vision—
But till the Merchant buy—
Still Fable—in the Isles of Spice—
The subtle Cargoes—lie—

At least—'tis Mutual—Risk—
Some—found it—Mutual Gain—
Sweet Debt of Life—Each Night to owe—
Insolvent—every Noon—

EMILY DICKINSON

Alter! When the Hills do—
Falter! When the Sun
Question if His Glory
Be the Perfect One—

Surfeit! When the Daffodil
Doth of the Dew—
Even as Herself—Sir—
I will—of You—

EMILY DICKINSON

The Good-morrow

I wonder, by my troth, what thou and I
Did, till we loved? Were we not weaned till then?
But sucked on country pleasures, childishly?
Or snored we in the seven sleepers' den?
'Twas so; but this, all pleasures fancies be.
If ever any beauty I did see,
Which I desired, and got, 'twas but a dream of thee.

And now good morrow to our waking souls,
Which watch not one another out of fear;
For love all love of other sights controls
And makes one little room an everywhere.
Let sea-discoverers to new worlds have gone,
Let maps to others worlds on worlds have shown,
Let us possess one world, each hath one, and is one.

My face in thine eye, thine in mine appears,
And true plain hearts do in the faces rest;
Where can we find two better hemispheres,
Without sharp North, without declining West.
Whatever dies was not mixed equally.
If our two loves be one, or thou and I
Love so alike that none do slacken, none can die.

JOHN DONNE

The reference to "the seven sleepers" presumes knowledge of an old Rip Van Winkle legend of seven early Christians who were immured in the persecution of 249 C.E. and who were believed to have slept for nearly two centuries. For the sake of comprehensibility, you might want to change this line to "Or snored we in some ancient wizard's den?"
    R. H.

from *The Anniversary*

All Kings, and all their favorites,
   All glory of honors, beauties, wits,
The sun itself, which makes times, as they pass,
Is elder by a year now than it was
When thou and I first one another saw:
All other things to their destruction draw,
   Only our love hath no decay;
This no tomorrow hath, nor yesterday,
Running it never runs from us away,
But truly keeps its first, last, everlasting day.

JOHN DONNE

A Wedding Song on St. Valentine's Day

Hail, Bishop Valentine, whose day this is,
   All the air is thy diocese,
   And all the chirping choristers
And other birds are thy parishioners;
     Thou marriest every year
The lyric lark, and the grave whispering dove,
The sparrow that neglects his life for love,
The household bird with the red stomacher,
    Thou mak'st the blackbird speed as soon
As doth the goldfinch, or the halcyon;
The husband cock looks out, and straight is sped,
And meets his wife, who brings her feather-bed.
This day more cheerfully than ever shine,
This day, which might enflame thyself, old Valentine.

Till now, thou warm'dst with multiplying loves
   Two larks, two sparrows, or two doves;
    All that is nothing unto this,
For thou this day couplest two Phoenixes;
     Thou mak'st a taper see
What the sun never saw, and what the Ark
(Which was of fowls and beasts the cage and park)
Did not contain, one bed contains, through thee,
    Two Phoenixes, whose joined breasts
Are unto one another mutual nests,
Where motion kindles such fires as shall give

Young Phoenixes, and yet the old shall live.

Whose love and courage never shall decline,

But make the whole year through, thy day, O Valentine.

JOHN DONNE
adapted by Robert Hass

The phoenix *is the mythological bird that dies and rises from its own ashes, a favorite Elizabethan metaphor for love-making. The* taper *is the bedroom candle, which witnesses the miracle.*
R. H.

An Epithalamion for Lawyers

Your learn'd identities untie
And in the nuptial bed (love's altar) lie
    A pleasing sacrifice; now dispossess
Yourselves of chains and robes which were put on
To adorn the day, not you; for you, alone,
    Like virtue and truth, are best in nakedness;
    This bed is only to the single state
A grave, but to a better one, a cradle;
Till now you were but able
    To be what now you are; so that you might
No longer say, *I may be*, but, *I am*,
    Tonight put on perfection and a lover's name.

JOHN DONNE
adapted by Robert Hass

*This is an excerpt from "Epithalamion Made at Lincoln's Inn." Lincoln's Inn is one
of the London law courts and also, in effect, the law school. So this is a marriage
poem for young professionals. The advice is to go naked—of status symbols. It
is nakedness, Donne, says, that both truth and the wedding night teach.*

    *The sense of the last sentence is "Tonight, so that you will not have to say
anymore* I may be *instead of* I am, *put on the perfection of your nakedness."*

    R. H.

*N*o love, to love of man and wife;
No hope, to hope of constant heart;
No joy, to joy in wedded life;
No faith, to faith in either part:
     Flesh is of flesh, and bone of bone
     When deeds and words and thoughts are one.

Thy friend an other friend may be,
But other self is not the same:
Thy spouse the self-same is with thee,
In body, mind, in goods and name:
     No thine, no mine, may other call,
     Now all is one, and one is all.

RICHARD EEDES

*T*his love is as good
as oil and honey to the throat,
as linen to the body,
as fine garments to the gods,
as incense to worshippers
when they enter in,
as the little seal-ring
to my finger.
It is like a ripe pear
in a man's hand,
it is like the dates
we mix with wine,
it is like the seeds
the baker adds to bread.
We will be together
even when old age comes.
And the days in between
will be food set before us,
dates and honey, bread and wine.

ANCIENT EGYPTIAN
from the translation of Michael V. Fox
(adapted by Robert Hass)

The text of this very old song dates from the 19th or 20th Egyptian dynasty (ca.
1300–1100 B.C.E.) and was found, with others, written in hieroglyphic on a vase.
The drink was probably not wine, but a beer spiced with dates. Beer-drinkers may
want to revise this version accordingly.
R. H.

from *Iphigeneia at Aulis*

Blessed are they
who share the delights of Aphrodite
and are not burned alive by them, moderate
and happy,
whom the passion has not stung into madness, at whom
the archer with golden hair,
Eros, has not aimed
desire in his two arrows, the one
striking rapture, the other
devastation. Oh Cyprian,
most beautiful of the goddesses, keep
such wild flights from me.
Let me know love
within reason, and desire within
marriage, and feel your presence
not your rage.
The natures of humans
are various, and human ways of acting
are different,
but everyone knows what is right,
and teaching
inclines them at last to virtue.
Humility is wisdom,
making us see the right way
as something beautiful.
And from this beauty honor is born
and life earns immortal fame.
It is a great thing, the pursuit of virtue:
at home, it is a stillness
in their love;

in the world, multiplied
ten thousand times among citizens,
it makes a city great.

EURIPIDES
translated by W. S. Merwin and George E. Dimock, Jr.

The Master Speed

No speed of wind or water rushing by
But you have speed far greater. You can climb
Back up a stream of radiance to the sky,
And back through history up the stream of time.
And you were given this swiftness, not for haste
Nor chiefly that you may go where you will,
But in the rush of everything to waste,
That you may have the power of standing still—
Off any still or moving thing you say.
Two such as you with such a master speed
Cannot be parted nor be swept away
From one another once you are agreed
That life is only life forevermore
Together wing to wing and oar to oar.

ROBERT FROST

The Creation

The woman and the man dreamed that God was dreaming about them.

God was singing and clacking his maracas as he dreamed his dream in a cloud of tobacco smoke, feeling happy but shaken by doubt and mystery.

The Makiritare Indians know that if God dreams about eating, he gives fertility and food. If God dreams about life, he is born and gives birth.

In their dream about God's dream, the woman and the man were inside a great shining egg, singing and dancing and kicking up a fuss because they were crazy to be born. In God's dream happiness was stronger than doubt and mystery. So dreaming, God created them with a song:

"I break this egg and the woman is born and the man is born. And together they will live and die. But they will be born again. They will be born again and die again and be born again. Because there is no death. They will never stop being born."

EDUARDO GALEANO
translated by Cedric Belfrage

The World

A man from a town of Negua, on the coast of Colombia, could climb
into the sky.

On his return, he described his trip. He told how he had contemplated
human life from on high. He said we are a sea of tiny flames.

Each person shines with his or her own light. No two flames are alike.
There are big flames and little flames, flames of every color. Some people's
flames are so still they don't even flicker in the wind while others have
wild flames that fill the air with sparks. Some foolish flames neither burn
nor shed light, but others blaze with life so fiercely that you can't look at
them without blinking and if you approach, you shine in fire.

EDUARDO GALEANO
translated by Cedric Belfrage

Whole Love

Every choice is always the wrong choice,
Every vote cast is always cast away—
How can truth hover between alternatives?

Then love me more than dearly, love me wholly,
Love me with no weighing of circumstance,
As I am pledged in honour to love you:

With no weakness, with no speculation
On what might happen should you and I prove less
Than bringers-to-be of our own certainty.
Neither was born by hazard: each foreknew
The extreme possession we are grown into.

ROBERT GRAVES

from *Everywhere Is Here*

By this exchange of eyes, this encirclement
You of me, I of you, together we baffle
Logic no doubt, but never understanding;
And laugh instead of choking back the tears
When we say goodbye.
                              Fog gathers thick about us
Yet a single careless pair of leaves, one green, one gold,
Whirl round and round each other skippingly
As though blown by a wind; pause and subside
In a double star, the gold above the green.

ROBERT GRAVES

*H*ere all seeking is over,
the lost has been found,
a mate has been found
to share the chills of winter—
now Love asks
that you be united.
Here is a place to rest,
a place to sleep,
a place in heaven.
Now two are becoming one,
the black night is scattered,
the eastern sky grows bright.
At last the great day has come!

HAWAIIAN SONG
from the translation of E. S. Craighill Handy and Mary Kawena Pukui
(adapted by Jane Hirshfield)

Love

Love bade me welcome; yet my soul drew back,
　　　　　Guilty of dust and sin.
But quick-eyed Love, observing me grow slack
　　　　　From my first entrance in,
Drew nearer to me, sweetly questioning,
　　　　　If I lacked any thing.

"A guest," I answered, "worthy to be here":
　　　　　Love said, "You shall be he."
"I the unkind, ungrateful? Ah my dear,
　　　　　I cannot look on thee."
Love took my hand, and smiling did reply,
　　　　　"Who made the eyes but I?"

"Truth, Lord, but I have marred them: let my shame
　　　　　Go where it doth deserve."
"And know you not," says Love, "who bore the blame?"
　　　　　"My dear, then I will serve."
"You must sit down," says Love, "and taste my meat":
　　　　　So I did sit and eat.

GEORGE HERBERT

Pale clouds, away! and welcome, day!
　　With night we banish sorrow:
Sweet air, blow soft! mount, lark, aloft!
　　To give my Love good-morrow;
Wings from the wind, to please her mind,
　　Notes from the lark I'll borrow.
Bird, prune thy wing! nightingale, sing!
　　To give my Love good-morrow.
　　To give my Love good-morrow
　　Notes from them all I'll borrow.

Wake from thy nest, robin redbreast!
　　Sing, birds, in every furrow!
And from each bill let music shrill
　　Give my fair Love good-morrow.
Blackbird and thrush, in every bush,
　　Stare, linnet, and cock-sparrow—　　　　　　Starling
You pretty elves, among yourselves
　　Sing my fair Love good-morrow!
　　To give my Love good-morrow
　　Sing, birds, in every furrow.

THOMAS HEYWOOD

You will probably have most fun with this rollicking Renaissance poem if several of the guests read it in chorus or in alternate lines.

*A*s I dig for wild orchids
in the autumn fields,
it is the deeply-bedded root
that I desire,
not the flower.

IZUMI SHIKIBU
translated by Jane Hirshfield with Mariko Aratani

*"Izumi Shikibu (974–1034) is recognized as the outstanding woman poet of
Japanese literature," Jane Hirshfield writes. "She lived in the imperial court during
the only golden age in literary history in which women writers were predominant."*

Butterfly Wine

The bride
    sips about one dewdrop
of the butterfly wine.

JAPANESE SONG
translated by R. H. Blyth

This is not a haiku, *but a* senryu, *the Japanese name for small, haiku-like poems
of social life. In the old Japanese marriage ceremony, two children—a "male
butterfly" and a "female butterfly"—pour wine into a cup from which both bride
and groom drink. The poem is probably intended to suggest a certain shyness on the
bride's part (or maybe downright reluctance). Our version might be "The bride /
takes one little bite / of the wedding-cake." We have included the senryu, really,
because we thought you might find the ritual gesture of the butterfly-children
interesting.*

    R. H.

I unpetalled you, like a rose,
to see your soul,
and I didn't see it.

But everything around
—horizons of lands and of seas—,
everything, out to the infinite,
was filled with a fragrance,
enormous and alive.

JUAN RAMÓN JIMÉNEZ
translated by Stephen Mitchell

To the bridge of love,
old stone between high cliffs
    —eternal meeting-place, red dusk—,
I come with my heart.
    —My beloved is only water,
which is always flowing, and doesn't deceive,
which is always flowing, and doesn't change,
which is always flowing, and doesn't end.

JUAN RAMÓN JIMÉNEZ
translated by Stephen Mitchell

*N*ow, bride and bridegroom, help to sing
The prize which Wedding here doth bring;
  And did so lately rap
  From forth the mother's lap
  To place you side by side,
  Where you must long abide
  That you may both ere day
  Rise perfect every way.

And, free from all the world and noise,
May you enjoy your mutual joys;
  Now you no fear controls
  But lips may mingle souls;
  And soft embraces bind
  To each the other's mind;
  Which may no power untie,
  Till one or both must die.

And Juno, whose great powers protect
The marriage bed, with good effect
  The labor of this night
  Bless thou, for future light:
  Let ivy not so bind
  As when their arms are twined:
  That they may both ere day
  Rise perfect every way.

BEN JONSON
adapted by Robert Hass

*T*he flute of interior time is played whether we hear it or not.
What we mean by "love" is its sound coming in.
When love hits the farthest edge of excess, it reaches a wisdom.
And the fragrance of that knowledge!
It penetrates our thick bodies,
it goes through walls—
Its network of notes has a structure as if a million suns were arranged
    inside.
This tune has truth in it.
Where else have you heard a sound like this?

KABIR
translated by Robert Bly

Wedding-Wind

The wind blew all my wedding-day,
And my wedding-night was the night of the high wind;
And a stable door was banging, again and again,
That he must go and shut it, leaving me
Stupid in candlelight, hearing rain,
Seeing my face in the twisted candlestick,
Yet seeing nothing. When he came back
He said the horses were restless, and I was sad
That any man or beast that night should lack
The happiness I had.

       Now in the day
All's ravelled under the sun by the wind's blowing.
He has gone to look at the floods, and I
Carry a chipped pail to the chicken-run,
Set it down, and stare. All is the wind
Hunting through clouds and forests, thrashing
My apron and the hanging cloths on the line.
Can it be borne, this bodying-forth by wind
Of joy my actions turn on, like a thread
Carrying beads? Shall I be let to sleep
Now this perpetual morning shares my bed?
Can even death dry up
These new delighted lakes, conclude
Our kneeling as cattle by the all-generous waters?

PHILIP LARKIN

from *Know Deeply, Know Thyself More Deeply*

Go deeper than love, for the soul has greater depths,
love is like the grass, but the heart is deep wild rock
molten, yet dense and permanent.

Go down to your deep old heart, and lose sight of yourself.
And lose sight of me, the me whom you turbulently loved.

Let us lose sight of ourselves, and break the mirrors.
For the fierce curve of our lives is moving again to the depths
out of sight, in the deep living heart

D. H. LAWRENCE

from *Fidelity*

Man and woman are like the earth, that brings forth flowers
in summer, and love, but underneath is rock.
Older than flowers, older than ferns, older than foraminiferae,
older than plasm altogether is the soul underneath.

And when, throughout all the wild chaos of love
slowly a gem forms, in the ancient, once-more-molten rocks
of two human hearts, two ancient rocks, a man's heart and a woman's,
that is the crystal of peace, the slow hard jewel of trust,
the sapphire of fidelity.
The gem of mutual peace emerging from the wild chaos of love.

D. H. LAWRENCE

The Ache of Marriage

The ache of marriage:

thigh and tongue, beloved,
are heavy with it,
it throbs in the teeth

We look for communion
and are turned away, beloved,
each and each

It is leviathan and we
in its belly
looking for joy, some joy
not to be known outside it

two by two in the ark of
the ache of it.

DENISE LEVERTOV

from *The Garden of Earthly Delights*

EARTH

Riding birds, feeling under our thighs the soft feathers
Of goldfinches, orioles, kingfishers,
Or spurring lions into a run, unicorns, leopards,
Whose coats brush against our nakedness,
We circle the vivid and abundant waters,
Mirrors from which emerge a man's and a woman's head,
Or an arm, or the round breasts of the sirens.
Every day is the day of berry harvest here.
The two of us bite into wild strawberries
Bigger than a man, we plunge into cherries,
We are drenched with the juices of their wine,
We celebrate the colors of carmine
And vermilion, as in toys on a Christmas tree.
We are many, a whole tribe swarming,
And so like each other that our lovemaking
Is as sweet and immodest as a game of hide-and-seek.
And we lock ourselves inside the crowns of flowers
Or in transparent, iridescent bubbles.
Meanwhile a flock of lunar signs fills the sky
To prepare the alchemical nuptials of the planets.

CZESLAW MILOSZ
translated by the author and Robert Hass

Adam and Eve in the Garden

Both turned, and under open sky adored
The God that made both Sky, Air, Earth, and Heaven,
Which they beheld, the Moon's resplendent globe,
And starry Pole: "Thou also mad'st the Night,
Maker Omnipotent, and thou the Day
Which we, in our appointed work employed,
Have finished, happy in our mutual help
And mutual love, the crown of all our bliss."
    This said unanimous, and other rites
Observing none, but adoration pure,
Which God likes best, into their inmost bower
Handed they went; and, eased the putting-off
These troublesome disguises which we wear,
Straight side by side were laid; nor turned, I ween,
Adam from his fair spouse, nor Eve the rites
Mysterious of connubial love refused.
Hail, wedded Love, mysterious law, true source
Of human offspring, sole propriety
In Paradise of all things common else!
By thee adulterous lust was driven from men
Among the bestial herds to range; by thee,
Founded in reason, loyal, just, and pure,
Relations dear, and all the charities
Of father, son, and brother, first were known.
Far be it that I should write thee sin or blame,
Or think thee unbefitting holiest place,
Perpetual fountain of domestic sweets,
Whose bed is undefiled and chaste pronounced,
Present, or past, as saints and patriarchs used.
Here Love his golden shafts employs, here lights
His constant lamp, and waves his purple wings.
    These, lulled by nightingales, embracing slept,

And on their naked limbs the flowery roof
Showered roses, which the morn repaired. Sleep on,
Blest pair, and O! yet happiest, if ye seek
No happier state, and know to know no more.

JOHN MILTON
adapted by Robert Hass

Traditionalists who would like to evoke the spirit of the Puritan founders of New England will find their text right here in Paradise Lost, *the great Puritan poet John Milton's description of Adam and Eve in the garden.*
    R. H.

The Night Chant

In the house made of dawn,
In the house made of twilight,
In the house made of dark cloud,
In the house made of rain and mist, pollen and grasshoppers,
Where the dark mist curtains the doorway
And the path there is on the rainbow,
Where the zigzag lightning stands high on top,
Where the he-rain stands high on top,
God of the wet earth,
With your moccasins of dark clouds, come to us,
With your mind enveloped in dark clouds, come to us,
With the dark thunder above you, come to us soaring,
With the massed clouds at your feet, come to us soaring,
With the far darkness made of dark clouds over your head, come to us
      soaring,
With the far darkness made of the rain and the mist over your head,
      come to us soaring,
With the zigzag lightning flung out high over your head,
With the rainbow hanging high over your head, come to us soaring,
With the far darkness made of the dark cloud on the ends of your
      wings,
With the far darkness made of the rain and the mist on the ends of
      your wings, come to us soaring,
With the zigzag lightning, with the rainbow hanging high on the ends
      of your wings, come to us soaring,
With the near darkness made of dark cloud of the rain and the mist,
      come to us,
With the darkness of the earth, come to us.

An abundance of clouds we desire, swollen with rain,
An abundance of growth we desire,
An abundance of pollen, an abundance of dew we desire.

Happily may the fair white corn, to the ends of the earth, come with you,
Happily may the fair yellow corn, blue corn, corn of all kinds, plants of all
    kinds, goods of all kinds, fine stone of all kinds, to the ends of the
    earth, come with you,
With these before you, may they come with you,
With these behind you, may they come with you,
Thus you accomplish your tasks.
The old men will be happy, seeing you coming.
The old women will be happy, seeing you coming,
The young men and young women will see you,
The children will see you,
The chiefs will see you,
Happily, as they scatter in all directions, they will see you.
Happily they will regard you as they come back home.
May their roads home be peaceful,
Happily may they all return,
Walking in beauty.
Walking with beauty before them,
Walking with beauty behind them,
With beauty above and about them.
It is finished in beauty.
It is finished in beauty.

NAVAJO SONG
from the translation of Washington Matthews
(adapted by Robert Hass)

from *Sonnet XII*

Loving is a journey with water and with stars,
with smothered air and abrupt storms of flour:
loving is a clash of lightning-bolts
and two bodies defeated by a single drop of honey.

Kiss by kiss I move across your small infinity,
your borders, your rivers, your tiny villages,
and the genital fire transformed into delight

runs through the narrow pathways of the blood
until it plunges down, like a dark carnation,
until it is and is no more than a flash in the night.

PABLO NERUDA
translated by Stephen Mitchell

from *Sonnet XLVIII*

Two happy lovers make one single bread,
one single drop of moonlight in the grass.
When they walk, they leave two shadows that merge,
and they leave one single sun blazing in their bed.

PABLO NERUDA
translated by Stephen Mitchell

Calling-One's-Own

Wake up! flowers of the forest, sky-climbing birds of the prairie.
Wake up! Wake up! surprising fawn-eyed one.
When you look upon me I am filled up, like flowers that drink the dew.
The breath of your mouth is the fragrance of flowers in the morning.
Your breath is their fragrance at evening in the moon-of-the-fading-
    leaves.
The red streams in my veins flow toward you
As the forest streams to the sun in the moon-of-bright-nights.
When you are beside me my heart sings; it is a branch, dancing.
Dancing before the wind-spirit in the moon-when-the-strawberries-
    ripen.
When you frown upon me, beloved, my heart grows dark—
A shining river the cloud shadows darken,
And then when you smile comes the sun and makes look like gold
The furrows the cold wind draws on the water's face.
Myself! Behold me! blood of my beating heart.
The earth smiles—the waters smile—even the sky of clouds smiles—
    but I,
I lose the way of smiling when you are not near.
Wake up! Wake up! my beloved.

OJIBWAY SONG
from the translation of Charles Fenno Thompson
(adapted by Robert Hass)

The Wedding Vow

I did not stand at the altar, I stood
at the foot of the chancel steps, with my beloved,
and the minister stood on the top step
holding the open Bible. The church
was wood, painted white inside, no people—God's
stable perfectly cleaned. It was night,
Spring, outside a moat of mud,
and inside, from the rafters, flies
fell onto the open Bible, and the minister
tilted it and brushed them off. We stood
beside each other, crying slightly
with fear and awe. In truth, we had married
that first night, in bed, we had been
married by our bodies, but now we stood
in history—what our bodies had said
mouth to mouth we now said publicly,
gathered together, *death*. We stood
holding each other by the hand, yet I also
stood as if alone, for a moment,
just before the vow, though taken
years before, took. It was a vow
of the present and the future, and yet I felt it
to have some touch on the distant past
or the distant past on it, I felt
the silent dry crying ghost of my
parents' marriage there, somewhere
in the bright space—perhaps one of the
plummeting flies, bouncing slightly
as it hit *forsaking all others*, then brushed
away. I felt as if I had come
to claim a promise—the sweetness I'd inferred
from their sourness; and I felt as if

I had come, congenitally unworthy, to beg.
And yet, I had been working toward this love
all my life. And then it was time
to speak—he was offering me, no matter
what, his life. That is all I had to
do, there, to accept that gift
I had longed for—to say I had accepted it,
as if being asked if I breathe. Do I take?
I do. I take as he takes—we have been
practicing this. Do you bear this pleasure? I do.

SHARON OLDS

The Knowing

Afterwards, when we have slept, paradise-
comaed, and woken, we lie a long time
looking at each other.
I do not know what he sees, but I see
eyes of surpassing tenderness
and calm, a calm like the dignity
of matter. I love the open ocean
blue-grey-green of his iris, I love
the curve of it against the white,
that curve the sight of what has caused me
to come, when he's quite still, deep
inside me. I have never seen a curve
like that, except the earth from outer
space. I don't know where he got
his kindness without self-regard,
almost without self, and yet
he chose one woman, instead of the others.
By knowing him, I get to know
the purity of the animal
which mates for life. Sometimes he is slightly
smiling, but mostly he just gazes at me gazing,
his entire face lit. I love
to see it change if I cry—there is no worry,
no pity, a graver radiance. If we
are on our backs, side by side,
with our faces turned fully to face each other,
I can hear a tear from my lower eye
hit the sheet, as if it is an early day on earth,
and then the upper eye's tears
braid and sluice down through the lower eyebrow
like the invention of farming, irrigation, a non-nomadic people.
I am so lucky that I can know him.

This is the only way to know him.
I am the only one who knows him.
When I wake again, he is still looking at me,
as if he is eternal. For an hour
we wake and doze, and slowly I know
that though we are sated, though we are hardly
touching, this is the coming the other
coming brought us to the edge of—we are entering,
deeper and deeper, gaze by gaze,
this place beyond the other places,
beyond the body itself, we are making
love.

SHARON OLDS

from *The First Letter to the Corinthians*

Though I speak in the tongues of men or of angels: if I have no love, I am
a clanging bell or a tinkling cymbal. Though I prophesy and see into all
the mysteries and all hidden knowledge, and have faith enough to move
mountains: if I have no love, I am nothing. And though I give away all
my possessions to feed the poor, and offer up my body to be burned: if I
have no love, I gain nothing.

Love is patient and kind, is never envious or boastful or conceited,
does not act rudely or selfishly, is not easily angered, does not count up
offenses, takes no pleasure in injustice, but rejoices in the truth; includes
all things, has faith in all things, hopes for all things, endures all things.

Love never ends. If there are prophecies, they will disappear; if there is
ecstasy, it will cease; if there is knowledge, it will vanish . . . But faith,
hope, and love remain forever, these three; and the greatest of these is
love.

PAUL OF TARSUS
translated by Stephen Mitchell

Wreath for a Bridal

What though green leaves only witness
Such pact as is made once only; what matter
That owl voice sole "yes," while cows utter
Low moos of approve; let sun surpliced in brightness
Stand stock still to laud these mated ones
Whose stark act all coming double luck joins.

Couched daylong in cloisters of stinging nettle
They lie, cut-grass assaulting each separate sense
With savor; coupled so, pure paragons of constance,
This pair seek single state from that dual battle.
Now speak some sacrament to parry scruple
For wedlock wrought within love's proper chapel.

Call here with flying colors all watchful birds
To people the twigged aisles; lead babel tongues
Of animals to choir: "Look what thresh of wings
Wields guard of honor over these!" Starred with words
Let night bless that luck-rooted mead of clover
Where, bedded like angels, two burn one in fever.

From this holy day on, all pollen blown
Shall strew broadcast so rare a seed on wind
That every breath, thus teeming, set the land
Sprouting fruit, flowers, children most fair in legion
To slay spawn of dragon's teeth: speaking this promise,
Let flesh be knit, and each step hence go famous.

SYLVIA PLATH

from *The Second Duino Elegy*

Lovers, gratified in each other, I am asking *you*
about us. You hold each other. Where is your proof?
Look, sometimes I find that my hands have become aware
of each other, or that my time-worn face
shelters itself inside them. That gives me a slight
sensation. But who would dare to exist, just for that?
You, though, who in each other's passion
grow until, overwhelmed, he begs you:
"No *more* . . ."; you who beneath his hands
swell with abundance, like autumn grapes;
you who may disappear because the other has wholly
emerged: I am asking *you* about us. I know,
you touch so blissfully because the caress preserves,
because the place you so tenderly cover
does not vanish; because underneath it
you feel pure duration. So you promise eternity, almost,
from the embrace. And yet, when you have survived
the terror of the first glances, the longing at the window,
and the first walk together, once only, through the garden:
lovers, *are* you the same? When you lift yourselves up
to each other's mouth and your lips join, drink against drink:
oh how strangely each drinker seeps away from his action.

Weren't you astonished by the caution of human gestures
on Attic gravestones? Wasn't love and departure
placed so gently on shoulders that it seemed to be made
of a different substance than in our world? Remember the hands,
how weightlessly they rest, though there is power in the torsos.

These self-mastered figures know: "We can go this far,
this is ours, to touch one another this lightly; the gods
can press down harder upon us. But that is the gods' affair."

RAINER MARIA RILKE
translated by Stephen Mitchell

from *The Third Duino Elegy*

No, we don't accomplish our love in a single year
as the flowers do; an immemorial sap
flows up through our arms when we love. Dear girl,
this: that we loved, inside us, not One who would someday appear, but
seething multitudes; not just a single child,
but also the fathers lying in our depths
like fallen mountains; also the dried-up riverbeds
of ancient mothers—; also the whole
soundless landscape under the clouded or clear
sky of its destiny—: all this, my dear, preceded you.

And you yourself, how could you know
what primordial time you stirred in your lover. What passions
welled up inside him from departed beings. What
women hated you there. How many dark
sinister men you aroused in his veins. Dead
children reached out to touch you . . . Oh gently, gently,
let him see you performing, with love, some confident daily task,—
lead him out close to the garden, give him what outweighs
the heaviest night . . . . . .
                Restrain him . . . . . .

RAINER MARIA RILKE
translated by Stephen Mitchell

from *The Seventh Duino Elegy*

Isn't the secret intent
of this taciturn earth, when it forces lovers together,
that inside their boundless emotion all things may shudder with joy?
Threshold: what it means for two lovers
to be wearing down, imperceptibly, the ancient threshold of their door—
they too, after the many who came before them
and before those to come . . . . , lightly.

RAINER MARIA RILKE
translated by Stephen Mitchell

The Sonnets to Orpheus I,4

O you tender ones, walk now and then
into the breath that blows coldly past.
Upon your cheeks let it tremble and part;
behind you it will tremble together again.

O you blessèd ones, you who are whole,
you who seem the beginning of hearts,
bows for the arrows and arrows' targets—
tear-bright, your lips more eternally smile.

Don't be afraid to suffer; return
that heaviness to the earth's own weight;
heavy are the mountains, heavy the seas.

Even the small trees you planted as children
have long since become too heavy; you could not
carry them now. But the winds . . . But the spaces . . .

RAINER MARIA RILKE
translated by Stephen Mitchell

The Sonnets to Orpheus I, 12

Hail to the god who joins us; for through him
arise the symbols where we truly live.
And, with tiny footsteps, the clocks move
separately from our authentic time.

Though we are unaware of our true status,
our actions stem from pure relationship.
Far away, antennas hear antennas
and the empty distances transmit . . .

Pure readiness. Oh unheard starry music!
Isn't your sound protected from all static
by the ordinary business of our days?

In spite of all the farmer's work and worry,
he can't reach down to where the seed is slowly
transmuted into summer. The earth *bestows*.

RAINER MARIA RILKE
translated by Stephen Mitchell

*M*y heart is like a singing bird
      Whose nest is in a watered shoot:
My heart is like an apple-tree
      Whose boughs are bent with thickset fruit;
My heart is like a rainbow shell
      That paddles in a halcyon sea;
My heart is gladder than all these
      Because my love is come to me.

Raise me a dais of silk and down;
      Hang it with vair and purple dyes;
Carve it in doves and pomegranates,
      And peacocks with a hundred eyes;
Work it in gold and silver grapes,
      In leaves and silver fleurs-de-lys;
Because the birthday of my life
      Is come, my love is come to me.

CHRISTINA ROSSETTI

*T*urn me like a waterwheel turning a millstone.
Plenty of water, Living Water.
Keep me in one place and scatter the love.
Leaf moves in a wind, straw drawn toward amber,
all parts of the world are in love,
but they do not tell their secrets: Cows grazing
on a sacramental table, ants whispering in Solomon's ear.
Mountains mumbling an echo. Sky, calm.
If the sun were not in love, he would have no brightness,
the side of the hill no grass on it.
The ocean would come to rest somewhere.

Be a lover as they are, that you come to know
your Beloved. Be faithful that you may know
Faith. The other parts of the universe did not accept
the next responsibility of love as you can.
They were afraid they might make a mistake
with it, the inspired knowing
that springs from being in love.

RUMI
translated by Coleman Barks with A. J. Arberry

*T*his marriage be wine with halvah, honey dissolving in milk.

This marriage be the leaves and fruit of a date tree.

This marriage be women laughing together for days on end.

This marriage, a sign for us to study.

This marriage, beauty.

This marriage, a moon in a light-blue sky.

This marriage, this silence fully mixed with spirit.

RUMI
translated by Coleman Barks with A. J. Arberry

Rumi wrote this poem for his son's wedding.

The minute I heard my first love story
I started looking for you, not knowing
how blind that was.

Lovers don't finally meet somewhere.
They're in each other all along.

RUMI
translated by Coleman Barks with John Moyne

Song for the Goddess of Love

Leave Crete,
Aphrodite,
and come to this
sacred place
encircled by apple trees,
fragrant with offered smoke.

Here, cold springs
sing softly
amid the branches;
the ground is shady with roses;
from trembling young leaves
a deep drowsiness pours.

In the meadow,
horses are cropping the wildflowers of spring,
scented fennel
blows on the breeze.

In this place,
Lady of Cyprus, pour
the nectar that honors you
into our cups,
gold, and raised for the drinking.

SAPPHO
adapted by Jane Hirshfield

The oldest wedding songs in the West are by Sappho of Lesbos, who lived in the seventh century B.C.E. *They exist only in fragments.*

    Aphrodite, the goddess of love, had her home on Crete. (Her cave can still be seen from the road into the White Mountains on the way to Samaria Gorge.)
    R. H.

Prothalamion for an Autumn Wedding

How pure the hearts of lovers as they walk
Through the rich quiet fields
Where the stiff wheat grows heavy on the stalk
And over barley and its paler golds
The air is bright—

They do not even walk yet hand in hand,
But every sense is pricked alive so sharp
That life breathes through them from the burning land
And they could use the wind itself for harp,
And oh, to drink the light!

Now all around them earth moves toward an end,
The gold turning to bronze, the barley tasseled,
The fruit stored up, and soon the sheaves will bend
Their heads together in the rich wedding-bed
All are about to enter.

The hearts of lovers as they walk, how pure;
How cool the wind upon the open palm
As they move on toward harvest, and so sure
Even this ripening has a marvelous calm
And a still center.

MAY SARTON

from *The Mind of Absolute Trust*

For the mind in harmony with the Tao,
    all selfishness disappears.
With not even a trace of self-doubt,
    you can trust the universe completely.
All at once you are free,
    with nothing left to hold on to.
All is empty, brilliant,
    perfect in its own being.
In the world of things as they are,
    there is no self, no non-self.
If you want to describe its essence,
    the best you can say is "Not-two."
In this "Not-two" nothing is separate,
    and nothing in the world is excluded.
The enlightened of all times and places
    have entered into this truth.
In it there is no gain or loss;
    one instant is ten thousand years.
There is no here, no there;
    infinity is right before your eyes.
The tiny is as large as the vast
    when objective boundaries have vanished;
the vast is as small as the tiny
    when you don't have external limits.
Being is an aspect of non-being;
    non-being is no different from being.
Until you understand this truth,
    you won't see anything clearly.
One is all; all
    are one. When you realize this,
    what reason for holiness or wisdom?
The mind of absolute trust

is beyond all thought, all striving,

is perfectly at peace, for in it

there is no yesterday, no today, no tomorrow.

SENG-TS'AN
adapted by Stephen Mitchell

The Chinese monk Seng-ts'an (?–606) was the Third Founding Teacher of Zen. Upon meeting the Second Founding Teacher, Hui-k'e, he said, "I beg you, Master, purify me of my sins." The Master said, "Bring me your sins, and I will purify you." After a long silence, Seng-ts'an said, "I have searched for my sins, but I can't find them anywhere." The Master said, "Then I have purified you." Upon hearing this, Seng-ts'an was enlightened.

This classic text points to a state of mind in which we are married not only to the beloved, but to the whole universe.

s. m.

Sonnet 116

Let me not to the marriage of true minds
Admit impediments. Love is not love
Which alters when it alteration finds,
Or bends with the remover to remove:
O, no! it is an ever-fixèd mark,
That looks on tempests and is never shaken;
It is the star to every wandering bark,
Whose worth's unknown, although its height be taken.
Love's not Time's fool, though rosy lips and cheeks
Within his bending sickle's compass come;
Love alters not with his brief hours and weeks
But bears it out even to the edge of doom.
  If this be error and upon me proved,
  I never writ, nor no man ever loved.

WILLIAM SHAKESPEARE

from *Romeo and Juliet*

Juliet: Good-night, good-night! as sweet repose and rest
Come to thy heart as that within my breast!
Romeo: O! wilt thou leave me so unsatisfied?
Juliet: What satisfaction canst thou have tonight?
Romeo: The exchange of thy love's faithful vow for mine.
Juliet: I gave thee mine before thou didst request it;
And yet I would it were to give again.
Romeo: Wouldst thou withdraw it? for what purpose, love?
Juliet: But to be frank, and give it thee again.
And yet I wish but for the thing I have:
My bounty is as boundless as the sea,
My love as deep; the more I give to thee,
The more I have, for both are infinite.

WILLIAM SHAKESPEARE

O fair! O sweet! when I do look on thee,
     In whom all joys so well agree,
Heart and soul do sing in me.
     Just accord all music makes;
In thee just accord excelleth,
Where each part in such peace dwelleth,
     One of other, beauty takes.
Since, then, truth to all minds telleth
     That in thee lives harmony,
     Heart and soul do sing in me.

O fair! O sweet! when I do look on thee,
     In whom all joys so well agree,
Heart and soul do sing in me.
     They that heaven have known do say,
That whoso that grace obtaineth,
To see what fair sight there reigneth,
     Forcèd are to sing alway:
So then, since that heaven remaineth
     In thy face I plainly see,
     Heart and soul do sing in me.

SIR PHILIP SIDNEY

You might want to divide these stanzas between two readers, male and female.

Long Their Coupled Joys Maintain

Let Mother Earth now deck herself in flowers,
    To see her offspring seek a good increase,
Where justest love has gathered Cupid's powers,
    And war of thoughts is swallowed up in peace,
        Which never may decrease,
        But, like the turtles fair,
        Live one in two, a well-united pair;
        Which that no charm may stain,
        O, long their coupled joys maintain!

O Heaven awake! show forth a shining face;
    Let not the slumb'ring clouds thy beauties hide,
But with thy cheerful presence help to grace
    The ardent bridegroom and the eager bride;
        Whose loves may ever bide,
        Like to the elm and vine,
        With mutual embracements them to twine,
        In which delightful pain,
        O, long their coupled joys maintain!

All churlish words, shrewd answers, crabbèd looks,
    All privateness, self-seeking, inward spite,
All waywardness, which nothing kindly brooks,
    All strife for toys and claiming other's right,
        Be hence, aye put to flight;
        All counting up of cost,
        Amounts conceded, given, got, or lost,
        Be fled, as things most vain:
        O, long their coupled joys maintain!

Virtue, if not a god, then God's chief part,
    Be thou the knot of this their open vow,

That they become each other's head and heart,
   He bow to her, she unto him do bow,
      Each other still allow,
      Like two well-planted trees:
      Deep roots, bright blossoms, fruit and falling leaves,
      In sun and battering rain,
      O, long their coupled joys maintain!

SIR PHILIP SIDNEY
adapted by Robert Hass

Now touch the air softly,
Step gently. One, two . . .
I'll love you till roses
Are robin's-egg blue;
I'll love you till gravel
Is eaten for bread,
And lemons are orange,
And lavender's red.

Now touch the air softly,
Swing gently the broom.
I'll love you till windows
Are all of a room;
And the table is laid,
And the table is bare,
And the ceiling reposes
On bottomless air.

I'll love you till Heaven
Rips the stars from his coat,
And the Moon rows away in
A glass-bottomed boat;
And Orion steps down
Like a diver below,
And Earth is ablaze,
And Ocean aglow.

So touch the air softly,
And swing the broom high.
We will dust the gray mountains,
And sweep the blue sky;
And I'll love you as long

As the furrow the plow,
As However is Ever,
And Ever is Now.

WILLIAM JAY SMITH

I have come into my garden,
My sister, my bride,
I have gathered the myrrh and spices,
I have eaten from the honeycomb,
I have drunk the milk and the wine.

Feast, friends, and drink
Till you are drunk with love!

THE SONG OF SONGS
translated by Chana and Ariel Bloch

*W*ake up, my love, my companion,
And come away!

Come, winter is over now,
The rains are done,
Wildflowers cover the fields.
Now is the time of the nightingale.
In every meadow you hear
The song of the turtle dove.

The fig tree has sweetened
Its new green fruit
And the young budded vines smell spicy.
Wake up, my love, my companion,
And come away.

THE SONG OF SONGS
translated by Chana and Ariel Bloch

Bind me as a seal upon your heart,
A sign upon your arm,

For love is as fierce as death,
Its jealousy bitter as the grave.
Even its sparks are a raging fire,
A devouring flame.

Great seas cannot extinguish love,
No river can sweep it away.

If a man tried to buy love
With all the wealth of his house,
He would be despised.

THE SONG OF SONGS
translated by Chana and Ariel Bloch

from *Epithalamion*

Now is this love already forth to come:
Let all the young girls therefore well await:
And ye fresh boys that tend upon the groom,
Prepare yourselves, for he is coming straight.
Set all your things in seemly good array,
Fit for so joyful day,
The joyful'st day that ever sun did see.
Fair sun! show forth thy favorable ray,
And let thy life-full heat not fervent be,
For fear of burning a sunshiny face,
Its beauty to disgrace.
O fairest Phoebus! father of the Muse!
If ever we did honor you aright,
Or sing the thing that might your mind delight,
Do not your servants' simple boon refuse;
But let this day, let this one day be theirs.
Let all the rest be yours.
Then we your sovereign praises loud will sing,
That all the woods shall answer, and their echo ring.

Open the temple gates unto their love,
Open them wide that they may enter in,
And all the posts adorn as doth behove,
And all the pillars deck with garlands trim,
For to receive them both with honor due,
When they come in to you.
With trembling steps and humble reverence
They have come in, before the Almighty's view;
Of them, young people, learn obedience,
When so you come into these holy places,
To humble your proud faces:
Bring them up to the high altar, that they may

The sacred ceremonies there partake,
The which do endless matrimony make,
And let the roaring organ loudly play
The praises of the Lord in lively notes,
While with melodious throats
The choristers the joyous anthem sing,
That all the woods may answer and their echo ring.

EDMUND SPENSER
adapted by Robert Hass

Spenser's is probably the most admired epithalamion in the English language. It was written for his own marriage, and it is quite long. This adaptation of two stanzas may also be too long to read. The second of the two stanzas is the soul of the poem and contains its most wonderful lines:

    The sacred ceremonies there partake,
    The which do endless matrimony make.

This is really the first European poem to move the meaning of the epithalamion from the bedroom to the altar, from the idea that the center of the ceremony is sexual consummation to the idea that the center of it is an eternal vow.

    R. H.

Re-statement of Romance

The night knows nothing of the chants of night.
It is what it is as I am what I am:
And in perceiving this I best perceive myself

And you. Only we two may interchange
Each in the other what each has to give.
Only we two are one, not you and night,

Nor night and I, but you and I, alone,
So much alone, so deeply by ourselves,
So far beyond the casual solitudes,

That night is only the background of our selves,
Supremely true each to its separate self,
In the pale light that each upon the other throws.

WALLACE STEVENS

I will make you brooches and toys for your delight,
Of bird-song at morning and star-shine at night.
I will build a palace fit for you and me,
Of green days in forests and blue days at sea.

I will make my kitchen, and you shall keep your room,
Where white flows the river and bright blows the broom,
And you shall wash your linen and keep your body white
In rainfall at morning and dewfall at night.

And this shall be for music when no one else is near,
The fine song for singing, the rare song to hear!
That only I remember, that only you admire,
Of the broad road that stretches and the roadside fire.

ROBERT LOUIS STEVENSON

Wedding Song: Lullaby for Sleepy Lovers

Hail bride and bridegroom, children both of Jove,
With fruitful joys let Hera bless your love!
Let Venus furnish you with full desires,
Add vigor to your wills and fuel your fires!
Let Jove, and luck, augment your wealthy store,
Give much to you, and to your children more!
From generous loins a generous race will spring,
Each girl will be a queen, each boy a king.
So sleep if sleep you can, but while you rest,
Sleep close, with folded arms, and breast to breast.
Rise in the morn, but oh! before you rise,
Do not neglect your morning exercise!
Just as, when night and winter disappear,
The purple morning, rising with the year,
Salutes the spring, so you, with wond'ring eyes,
Should light the world and brighten all the skies!

THEOCRITUS
translated by John Dryden
(and adapted by Robert Hass)

This rowdy and good-humored piece is taken from an adaptation of the third-century B.C.E. poet Theocritus by the seventeenth-century English poet John Dryden. Lots of the classical epithalamions linger over the thought of the wedding night more heartily than modern taste is likely to feel comfortable with in a public reading. But this one has a certain charm: it cheerfully calls on all the gods for their blessing and urges the lovers to be sure to use not just the night but the morning to best advantage.

  R. H.

from *When I Heard at the Close of Day*

The day when I rose at dawn from the bed of perfect health, refresh'd,
    singing, inhaling the ripe breath of autumn,
When I saw the full moon in the west grow pale and disappear in the
    morning light,
When I wander'd alone over the beach, and undressing bathed, laughing
    with the cool waters, and saw the sun rise,
And when I thought how my dear friend my lover was on his way
    coming, O then I was happy,
O then each breath tasted sweeter, and all that day my food nourish'd
    me more, and the beautiful day pass'd well,
And the next came with equal joy, and with the next at evening came
    my friend,
And that night while all was still I heard the waters roll slowly
    continually up the shores,
I heard the hissing rustle of the liquid and sands as directed to me
    whispering to congratulate me,
For the one I love most lay sleeping by me under the same cover in the
    cool night,
In the stillness in the autumn moonbeams his face was inclined toward me,
And his arm lay lightly around my breast—and that night I was happy.

WALT WHITMAN

Marriage

So different, this man
And this woman:
A stream flowing
In a field.

WILLIAM CARLOS WILLIAMS

The Rewaking

Sooner or later
we must come to the end
of striving

to re-establish
the image the image of
the rose

but not yet
you say extending the
time indefinitely

by
your love until a whole
spring

rekindle
the violet to the very
lady's-slipper

and so by
your love the very sun
itself is revived

WILLIAM CARLOS WILLIAMS

*W*here will you and I sleep?
At the down-turned jagged rim of the sky
You and I will sleep.
You and I will sleep together.

WINTU SONG
from the translation of Dorothy Demetracopoulou
(adapted by Robert Hass)

A Blessing

Just off the highway to Rochester, Minnesota,
Twilight bounds softly forth on the grass.
And the eyes of those two Indian ponies
Darken with kindness.
They have come gladly out of the willows
To welcome my friend and me.
We step over the barbed wire into the pasture
Where they have been grazing all day, alone.
They ripple tensely, they can hardly contain their happiness
That we have come.
They bow shyly as wet swans. They love each other.
There is no loveliness like theirs.
At home once more,
They begin munching the young tufts of spring in the darkness.
I would like to hold the slenderer one in my arms,
For she has walked over to me
And nuzzled my left hand.
She is black and white,
Her mane falls wild on her forehead,
And the light breeze moves me to caress her long ear
That is delicate as the skin over a girl's wrist.
Suddenly I realize
That if I stepped out of my body I would break
Into blossom.

JAMES WRIGHT

I want to be your friend
for ever and ever.
When the hills are all flat
and the rivers are all dry,
when the trees blossom in winter
and the snow falls in summer,
when heaven and earth mix—
not till then will I part from you.

THE YÜEH-FU
adapted from the translation of Arthur Waley

*In the country of Yüeh, when two people became friends they set up an altar of
earth, made sacrifices on it, and recited this oath.*

LONGER
READINGS

from *Poetry and Marriage*

The meaning of marriage begins in the giving of words. We cannot join ourselves to one another without giving our word. And this must be an unconditional giving, for in joining ourselves to one another we join ourselves to the unknown. We can join one another *only* by joining the unknown. We must not be misled by the procedures of experimental thought: in life, in the world, we are never given two known results to choose between, but only *one* result that we choose without knowing what it is.

Marriage rests upon the immutable *givens* that compose it: words, bodies, characters, histories, places. Some wishes cannot succeed; some victories cannot be won; some loneliness is incorrigible. But there is relief and freedom in knowing what is real; these givens come to us out of the perennial reality of the world, like the terrain we live on. One does not care for this ground to make it a different place, or to make it perfect, but to make it inhabitable and to make it better. To flee from its realities is only to arrive at them unprepared.

Because the condition of marriage is worldly and its meaning communal, no one party to it can be solely in charge. What you alone think it ought to be, it is not going to be. Where you alone think you want it to go, it is not going to go. It is going where the two of you—and marriage, time, life, history, and the world—will take it. You do not know the road; you have committed your life to a way.

Forms join us to time, to the consequences and fruitions of our own passing. The Zen student, the poet, the husband, the wife—none knows with certainty what he or she is staying for, but all know the likelihood that they will be staying "a while": to find out what they are staying for. And it is the faith of all of these disciplines that they will not stay to find that they should not have stayed.

That faith has nothing to do with what is usually called optimism. As the traditional marriage ceremony insists, not everything that we stay to find out will make us happy. The faith, rather, is that by staying, and only by staying, we will learn something of the truth, that the truth is good to know, and that it is always both different and larger than we thought.

WENDELL BERRY

from *Love*

Personal beauty is then first charming and itself when it dissatisfies us with any end; when it becomes a story without an end; when it suggests gleams and visions and not earthly satisfactions; when it makes the beholder feel his unworthiness; when he cannot feel more right to it than to the firmament and the splendors of a sunset.

Hence arose the saying, "If I love you, what is that to you?" We say so because we feel that what we love is not in your will, but above it. It is not you, but your radiance. It is that which you know not in yourself and can never know.

This agrees well with that high philosophy of Beauty which the ancient writers delighted in; for they said that the soul of man, embodied here on earth, went roaming up and down in quest of that other world of its own out of which it came into this, but was soon stupefied by the light of the natural sun, and unable to see any other objects than those of this world, which are but shadows of real things. Therefore the Deity sends the glory of youth before the soul, that it may avail itself of beautiful bodies as aids to its recollection of the celestial good and fair; and the man beholding such a person in the female sex runs to her and finds the highest joy in contemplating the form, movement and intelligence of this person, because it suggests to him the presence of that which indeed is within the beauty, and the cause of the beauty.

If however, from too much conversing with material objects, the soul was gross, and misplaced its satisfaction in the body, it reaped nothing but sorrow; body being unable to fulfil the promise which beauty holds out; but if, accepting the hint of these visions and suggestions which beauty makes to his mind, the soul passes through the body and falls to admire strokes of character, and the lovers contemplate one another in their discourses and their actions, then they pass to the true palace of beauty, more and more inflame their love of it, and by this love extinguishing the base affection, as the sun puts out fire by shining on the hearth, they become pure and hallowed. By conversation with that which is in itself excellent, magnanimous, lowly, and just, the lover comes to a warmer love of these nobilities, and a quicker apprehension of them. Then he passes from loving them in one to loving them in all, and so is the one beautiful soul only the door through which he enters to the society of all true and pure souls. In the particular society of his mate he attains a clearer sight of any spot, any taint which her beauty has contracted from this world, and is able to point it out and this with mutual joy that they are now able, without offense, to indicate blemishes and hindrances in each other, and give to each all help and comfort in curing the same. And beholding in many souls the traits of the divine beauty, and separating in each soul that which is divine from the taint which it has contracted in the world, the lover ascends to the highest beauty, to the love and knowledge of the Divinity, by steps on this ladder of created souls.

Little think the youth and maiden who are glancing at each other across crowded rooms with eyes so full of mutual intelligence, of the precious fruit long hereafter to proceed from this new, quite external stimulus. The work of vegetation begins first in the irritability of the bark and leaf-buds. From exchanging glances, they advance to acts of courtesy, of gallantry, then to fiery passion, to plighting troth and marriage. Passion beholds its object as a perfect unit. The soul is wholly embodied, and the body is wholly ensouled. Romeo, if dead, should be cut up into little stars to make the heavens fine. Life, with this pair, has no other aim, asks no more, than Juliet,—than Romeo. Night, day, studies, talents, kingdoms, religion, are all contained in this form full of soul, in this soul which is all form. The lovers delight in endearments, in avowals of love, in comparisons of their regards. When alone, they solace themselves with the remembered image of the other. Does that other see the same star, the same melting cloud, read the same book, feel the same emotion, that now delights me? They try and weigh their affection, and adding up costly advantages, friends, opportunities, properties, exult in discovering that willingly, joyfully, they would give all as a ransom for the beautiful, the beloved head, not one hair of which shall be harmed. But the lot of humanity is on these children. Danger, sorrow, and pain arrive to them as to us all. Love prays. It makes covenants with Eternal Power in behalf of this dear mate. The union which is thus effected and which adds a new value to every atom in nature—for it transmutes every thread throughout the whole web of relation into a golden ray, and bathes the soul in a new and sweeter element—is yet a temporary state. Not always can flowers, pearls, poetry, protestations, nor even home in another heart, content the awful soul that dwells in clay. It arouses itself at last from these endearments, as toys, and puts on the harness and aspires to vast and universal aims. The soul which is in the soul of each, craving a perfect beatitude, detects incongruities, defects and disproportion in the behavior of the other. Hence arise surprise, expostulation and pain. Yet that which drew them to each other was signs of loveliness, signs of virtue; and these virtues are there, however eclipsed. They appear and reappear and continue to attract; but the regard changes, quits the sign and attaches to the substance. This repairs the wounded affection. Meantime, as life wears on, it proves a game of permutation and combination of all possible positions of the parties, to employ all the resources of each and acquaint each with the strength and weakness of the other. For it is the nature and end of this relation, that they should represent the human race to each other. All that is in the world, which is or ought to be known, is cunningly wrought into the texture of man, of woman.

The world rolls; the circumstances vary every hour. The angels that inhabit this temple of the body appear at the windows, and the gnomes and vices also. By all the virtues they are united. If there be virtue, all the vices are known as such; they confess and flee. Their once flaming regard is sobered by time in either breast, and losing in violence what it gains in extent, it becomes a thorough good understanding. They resign each other without complaint to the good offices which man and woman are severally appointed to discharge in time, and exchange the passion which once could not lose sight of its object, for a cheerful disengaged furtherance, whether present or absent, of each other's designs. At last they discover that all which at first drew them together,—those once sacred features, that magical play of charms,—was deciduous, had a prospective end, like the scaffolding by which the house was built; and the purification of the intellect and the heart from year to year is the real marriage, foreseen and prepared from the first, and wholly above their consciousness. Looking at these aims with which two persons, a man and a woman, so variously and correlatively gifted, are shut up in one house to spend in the nuptial society forty or fifty years, I do not wonder at the emphasis with which the heart prophesies this crisis from early infancy, at the profuse beauty with which the instincts deck the nuptial bower, and nature and intellect and art emulate each other in the gifts and the melody they bring to the epithalamium.

Thus are we put in training for a love which knows not sex, nor person, nor partiality, but which seeks virtue and wisdom. We are by nature observers, and thereby learners. That is our permanent state. But we are often made to feel that our affections are but tents of a night. Though slowly and with pain, the objects of the affections change, as the objects of thought do. There are moments when the affections rule and absorb the man and make his happiness dependent on a person or persons. But in health the mind is presently seen again,—its overarching vault, bright with galaxies of immutable lights, and the warm loves and fears that swept over us as clouds must lose their finite character and blend with God, to attain their own perfection. But we need not fear that we can lose anything by the progress of the soul. The soul may be trusted to the end. That which is so beautiful and attractive as these relations, must be succeeded and supplanted only by what is more beautiful, and so on for ever.

RALPH WALDO EMERSON

These words of our great American sage may seem too Platonic, too ethical, for some people's taste. But Emerson is pointing beyond romantic love. When we fall in love with someone, what we are really falling in love with—within her physical beauty, within the beauty of her character—is the radiance of our own true nature.

The Tao of marriage doesn't lead two people to each other. They are each other's paths to themselves. The most important sentences in this essay describe the experience of every couple who have found in marriage their most intense spiritual practice:

"And so is the one beautiful soul only the door through which he enters to the society of all true and pure souls. In the particular society of his mate he attains a clearer sight of any spot, any taint which her beauty has contracted from this world, and is able to point it out and this with mutual joy that they are now able, without offense, to indicate blemishes and hindrances in each other, and give to each all help and comfort in curing the same."

S. M.

from *The Imitation of Christ*

Love is a great thing, a great good in every way; it alone lightens what is heavy, and leads smoothly over all roughness. For it carries a burden without being burdened, and makes every bitter thing sweet and tasty. Love wants to be lifted up, not held back by anything low. Love wants to be free, and far from all worldly desires, so that its inner vision may not be dimmed and good fortune bind it or misfortune cast it down. Nothing is sweeter than love; nothing stronger, nothing higher, nothing wider; nothing happier, nothing fuller, nothing better in heaven and earth; for love is born of God, and can find rest only in God, beyond all created things.

Love flies, runs, and rejoices; it is free and nothing can hold it back. It gives all for all, and has all in all, because it rests in the highest good, from whom all goodness originates and flows. It doesn't look to the gifts, but to the giver of all good things. Love often knows no limits, but burns beyond every limit. Love feels no burden, shrinks from no effort, aims beyond its strength, sees nothing as impossible, for it believes that all things are possible and allowable to it. Thus it is capable of everything, and it succeeds because it is confident of the result, while someone without love loses courage and gives up.

Love keeps watch and is never unaware, even when it sleeps; tired, it is never exhausted; hindered, it is never defeated; alarmed, it is never afraid; but like a living flame and a burning torch it bursts upward and blazes forth. Whoever loves, knows what this voice cries out; a mighty cry in the ears of God is the burning desire of the soul, which says:

"My love, you are all mine and I am all yours. Let me grow in love, so that I may learn to taste in my innermost heart how sweet it is to love, to be dissolved and to plunge into the ocean of love. Let love possess me; let me pass beyond myself in fervor and astonishment; let me sing love's song; let me follow my beloved into the heights; let my soul, rejoicing in love, lose itself in your praise. Let me love you more than myself; and myself only for you; and in you, all who truly love you, as love's law, shining from you, commands."

Love is quick, sincere, dutiful, joyous, and pleasant; brave, patient, faithful, prudent, serene, and vigorous; and it never seeks itself. For whenever we seek ourselves, we fall away from love. Love is watchful, humble, and upright; not weak, or frivolous, or directed toward vain things; temperate, pure, steady, calm, and alert in all the senses. Love is devoted and thankful to God, always trusting and hoping in him, even when it doesn't taste his sweetness, for without pain no one can live in love.

A lover must willingly accept every hardship and bitterness for the sake of the beloved, and must never turn away from the beloved when misfortune comes. Whoever isn't prepared to endure everything, and to abide in the will of the beloved, is unworthy to be called a lover.

THOMAS À KEMPIS
translated by Stephen Mitchell

from *Women in Love*

"I can't say it is love I have to offer—and it isn't love I want. It is something much more impersonal and harder—and rarer."

There was a silence, out of which she said:

"You mean you don't love me?"

She suffered furiously, saying that.

"Yes, if you like to put it like that. Though perhaps that isn't true. I don't know. At any rate, I don't feel the emotion of love for you—no, and I don't want to. Because it gives out in the last issues."

"Love gives out in the last issues?" she asked, feeling numb to the lips.

"Yes, it does. At the very last, one is alone, beyond the influence of love. There is a real impersonal me, that is beyond love, beyond any emotional relationship. So it is with you. But we want to delude ourselves that love is the root. It isn't. It is only the branches. The root is beyond love, a naked kind of isolation, an isolated me, that does *not* meet and mingle, and never can."

She watched him with wide, troubled eyes. His face was incandescent in its abstract earnestness.

"And you mean you can't love?" she asked, in trepidation.

"Yes, if you like. I have loved. But there is a beyond, where there is not love."

She could not submit to this. She felt it swooning over her. But she could not submit.

"But how do you know—if you have never *really* loved?" she asked.

"It is true what I say; there is a beyond, in you, in me, which is further than love, beyond the scope, as stars are beyond the scope of vision, some of them."

"Then there is no love," Ursula cried.

"Ultimately, no, there is something else. But, ultimately, there *is* no love."

Ursula was given over to this statement for some moments. Then she half rose from her chair, saying, in a final, repellent voice:

"Then let me go home—what am I doing here?"

"There is the door," he said. "You are a free agent."

He was suspended finely and perfectly in this extremity. She hung motionless for some seconds, then she sat down again.

"If there is no love, what is there?" she cried, almost jeering.

"Something," he said, looking at her, battling with his soul, with all his might.

"What?"

He was silent for a long time, unable to be in communication with her while she was in this state of opposition.

"There is," he said, in a voice of pure abstraction, "a final me which is stark and impersonal and beyond responsibility. So there is a final you. And it is there I would want to meet you—not in the emotional, loving plane—but there beyond, where there is no speech and no terms of agreement. There we are two stark, unknown beings, two utterly strange creatures, I would want to approach you, and you me. And there could be no obligation, because there is no standard for action there, because no understanding has been reaped from that plane. It is quite inhuman—so there can be no calling to book, in any form whatsoever—because one is outside the pale of all that is accepted, and nothing known applies. One can only follow the impulse, taking that which lies in front, and responsible for nothing, asked for nothing, giving nothing, only each taking according to the primal desire."

Ursula listened to this speech, her mind dumb and almost senseless, what he said was so unexpected and so untoward.

"It is just purely selfish," she said.

"If it is pure, yes. But it isn't selfish at all. Because I don't *know* what I want of you. I deliver *myself* over to the unknown, in coming to you, I am without reserves or defenses, stripped entirely, into the unknown. Only there needs the pledge between us, that we will both cast off everything, cast off ourselves even, and cease to be, so that that which is perfectly ourselves can take place in us."

She pondered along her own line of thought.

"But it is because you love me, that you want me?" she persisted.
"No it isn't. It is because I believe in you."

D. H. LAWRENCE

from *The Sacred Marriage of Shiva and Parvati*

On the marriage platform made of gold,
    embedded with gems that shone brightly, dispelling the darkness,
        Parvati sat with the beautiful Shiva.
It was as though a vine with blooming flowers
    sat entwined around the Wish-granting Tree
        on the top of Mount Meru, where the sun circles day and night.
If they took separate forms: the note and enchanting music,
    water and its coolness, milk and its sweet taste,
        the flower and its fragrance, the jewel and its luster;
if they took separate forms, and were seated like a man and a woman,
    then would they be like Shiva and the Mother
        who gave birth to the worlds.
The gods in the heavens, those from the eight directions,
    those who dwell in the underworlds, people on earth,
        and others, too—all these were gathered together in the marriage
            pavilion
    as though music had joined with its notes
and the noble sounds coming forth had achieved release,
becoming one with the holy feet of Shiva.
Then the god who holds in his beautiful hand the discus
    washed with water from a golden pot the holy red feet
        of the Dancing Lord who once appeared
           as a great red shining pillar of fire.
Anointing Shiva with sandalwood paste and pure, fragrant flowers,
    worshipping Him with lighted camphor,
        and performing the lighted-lamp ceremony with devotion,
           Vishnu stood in the presence of Shiva's boundless grace.
The holy water that dripped from the feet of the Lord,
    known in the Vedas to be the first brahmin among deities,
        was received by Brahma,

who lives in the lotus flower,
    by Vishnu, all the sages, by Indra and the other gods,
      by Nandin and his servants with him, as well as other devotees.
They took it, sprinkled it on their bodies, drank it,
    purifying themselves within and without.
Standing on one side, Vishnu took the hand of the goddess,
    a hand which is like the white bloom of the kantal flower,
      and placed it into the holy, red, lotus-flower-like hand of the
        Great One.
As mantras were chanted, Vishnu poured water onto their hands
    from a pot, while celestials poured down showers of blossoms
    as they watched in reverence.
Celestial courtesans danced;
    heavenly musicians sang music sweet as nectar;
Sages worshipped the couple, shouting "Hara, Hara!"
Gods were overwhelmed, covered with goosebumps;
servants raised folded arms over their heads and worshipped.
All were drowning in a sea of marriage bliss.
Gods, sages, and all the others were sinking in a flood of joy:
    speaking words of blessing with their pure tongues,
      sprinkling pearl-white rice soaked in kunkumam water
      at the feet of the One versed in the Vedas,
        that One who treated as flowers
          even the stones thrown by Puttanar.
"The Mother and the Father, though inseparable
    as the fragrance from the flower,
      by means of their own gracious sacred game
        seemed to us all for some time to be separate, apart
    and then graciously married,
    redeeming all three of the worlds,"
they said joyously among themselves.
Sweet milk given by the beautiful Wish-giving Cow,
    fruit provided by the Wish-giving Tree, ghee, sugar:
      all these things were mixed together in a pleasing taste,

then placed in a round, golden vessel with legs and offered
to the One who wears the laburnam garland dripping with honey.
"Take this," they prayed of Him.
The One who has eight forms
    touched the golden vessel, appearing to consume its contents,
        and to be happy with it.
He smiled brightly with His red mouth
    which is like the fragrant, blossoming ampal flower.
Lakshmi, Sarasvati, and chaste wives of other sages
    began singing auspicious songs.
The Lord Brahma of the sweet-smelling lotus
    sat beside the fire with all his sons.
The central tongue of the fire twisted, rising to taste
    the clarified butter poured from a mango-leaf ladle,
        and the divine red fire grew, turning as it swallowed
            the offering, sizzling in loud satisfaction.
As the four Vedas chanted,
    conch shells and musical instruments played.
Brahma, the well-versed, four-faced One,
    had flawlessly completed the sacrificial rituals
        according to the basic texts.
That great Yogi who graciously gives release
    to those without attachments
        tied the marriage necklace on the neck of Her
            who gave birth to the entire universe,
                and then He took Her red hand.
He it is who has tongues of fire,
    who makes the fire grow with flame,
        who receives the offerings poured into fire:
            He is all these things.
To plunge the world into the great joy of coupling,
    He became both man and woman
        and graciously performed the act of marrying.
Who can comprehend the acts of a Lord who does all this for us?

Then that great Lord with the moon in His hair,
    together with His Wife, received puffed rice in His hands
        and sprinkled it into the red flames.
To sages versed in the Vedas
    who know His holy form constitutes all things,
        They gave appropriate gifts, satisfying them fully
            and then, according to tradition,
                They walked together around the fire.
Then the Lord taking in His hand
    Parvati's lotus-flower foot, with its chiming anklets,
        placed it upon an auspiciously decorated grinding stone
            adorned with pure gold
                as He chanted the mantras.
"Where is the wife of the meritorious Vasishtha?" He asked.
With her red hands folded in praise she came forward
    as He bestowed upon her His gracious gaze.
In this way, without departing from the rules,
    all the sacrificial rituals were completed.
Then, as an example to the people
    of this world surrounded by roaring seas,
        while the four Vedas chanted,
    and women with bright teeth like pearls sang greetings,
the Lord who burned the god of love
    with the Lady whose forehead is like the moon,
        entered the nuptial chamber.
People, their eyes unblinking as they gazed
    at the Lord's auspicious form,
        were like pure heavenly beings.
Were they then worthy of worship?
Those who have achieved the prolonged gracious gaze of our Father:
    are they not worthy to receive gifts of cool flowers,
        praise, worship, and service, even from the gods?
Humans and gods: together they stood enthralled,
    side by side, no differences among them,

having viewed the wedding that relieves all suffering.
When the gracious gaze of the Lord with a third eye
  who dances in cremation grounds,
    relieves the suffering of birth in this world,
are not those of this world and those of the world above the same?

PARAÑCOTI MUNIVAR
translated by William P. Harman

*No tradition has elaborated the idea of sacred marriage more completely than
the Indian. In fact, for Hindu thought, as one scholar has said, the metaphor of
marriage is the meaning of this world. Here is an excerpt, teeming with life, from
an extraordinary seventeenth-century Tamil poem from South India about the
marriage of Shiva, god of gods, source of all wisdom, to Parvati, the mother of the
universe. Parvati has taken the form, in this poem, of the daughter of a legendary
king of the city of Madurai, so this is also a city-founding poem, that is, it is about
marriage as the basis of civilization as well as the joy and energy at the center of
physical and spiritual life. Even this excerpt, as you will see, is overwhelmingly
lush, intensely imagined, detail by detail. It is perhaps the fullest and most richly
articulated imagination of this idea of marriage in all of literature.*
    R. H.

from *Letters to a Young Poet*

Most people have turned their solutions toward what is easy and toward
the easiest side of the easy; but it is clear that we must trust in what is
difficult; everything alive trusts in it, everything in Nature grows and
defends itself any way it can and is spontaneously itself, tries to be itself
at all costs and against all opposition. We know little, but that we must
trust in what is difficult is a certainty that will never abandon us; it is good
to be solitary, for solitude is difficult; that something is difficult must be
one more reason for us to do it.

It is also good to love: because love is difficult. For one human being
to love another human being: that is perhaps the most difficult task that
has been entrusted to us, the ultimate task, the final test and proof, the
work for which all other work is merely preparation. That is why young
people, who are beginners in everything, are not yet *capable* of love: it is
something they must learn. With their whole being, with all their forces,
gathered around their solitary, anxious, upward-beating hearts, they
must learn to love. But learning-time is always a long, secluded time, and
therefore loving, for a long time ahead and far on into life, is—: solitude,
a heightened and deepened kind of aloneness for the person who loves.
Loving does not at first mean merging, surrendering, and uniting with
another person (for what would a union be of two people who are un-
clarified, unfinished, and still incoherent—?), it is a high inducement
for the individual to ripen, to become something in himself, to become
world, to become world in himself for the sake of another person; it is a
great, demanding claim on him, something that chooses him and calls
him to vast distances. Only in this sense, as the task of working on them-
selves, may young people use the love that is given to them. Merging
and surrendering and every kind of communion is not for them (who
must still, for a long, long time, save and gather themselves); it is the
ultimate, is perhaps that for which human lives are as yet barely large
enough. . . .

Whoever looks seriously will find that neither for death, which is
difficult, nor for difficult love has any clarification, any solution, any hint

of a path been perceived; and for both these tasks, which we carry wrapped up and hand on without opening, there is no general, agreed-upon rule that can be discovered. But in the same measure in which we begin to test life as individuals, these great Things will come to meet us, the individuals, with greater intimacy. The claims that the difficult work of love makes upon our development are greater than life, and we, as beginners, are not equal to them. But if we nevertheless endure and take this love upon us as burden and apprenticeship, instead of losing ourselves in the whole easy and frivolous game behind which people have hidden from the most solemn solemnity of their being,—then a small advance and a lightening will perhaps be perceptible to those who come long after us. That would be much.

We are only just now beginning to consider the relation of one individual to a second individual objectively and without prejudice, and our attempts to live such relationships have no model before them. And yet in the changes that time has brought about there are already many things that can help our timid novitiate.

The girl and the woman, in their new, individual unfolding, will only in passing be imitators of male behavior and misbehavior and repeaters of male professions. After the uncertainty of such transitions, it will become obvious that women were going through the abundance and variation of those (often ridiculous) disguises just so that they could purify their own essential nature and wash out the deforming influences of the other sex. Women, in whom life lingers and dwells more immediately, more fruitfully, and more confidently, must surely have become riper and more human in their depths than light, easygoing man, who is not pulled down beneath the surface of life by the weight of any bodily fruit and who, arrogant and hasty, undervalues what he thinks he loves. This humanity of woman, carried in her womb through all her suffering and humiliation, will come to light when she has stripped off the conventions of mere femaleness in the transformations of her outward status, and those men who do not yet feel it approaching will be astonished by it. Someday there will be girls and women whose name will no longer mean the mere opposite of the male, but something in itself, something that makes one think not of any complement, but only of life and reality: the female human being.

This advance (at first very much against the will of the outdistanced men) will transform the love experience, which is now filled with error, will change it from the ground up, and reshape it into a relationship that is meant to be between one human being and another, no longer one that flows from man to woman. And this more human love (which will fulfill itself with infinite consideration and gentleness, and kindness and clarity in binding and releasing) will resemble what we are now preparing painfully and with great struggle: the love that consists in this: that two solitudes protect and border and greet each other.

RAINER MARIA RILKE
translated by Stephen Mitchell

from *Letters*

Marriage is in many ways a simplification of life, and it naturally combines the strengths and wills of two young people so that, together, they seem to reach farther into the future than they did before. Above all, marriage is a new task and a new seriousness,—a new demand on the strength and generosity of each partner, and a great new danger for both.

The point of marriage is not to create a quick commonality by tearing down all boundaries; on the contrary, a good marriage is one in which each partner appoints the other to be the guardian of his solitude, and thus they show each other the greatest possible trust. A merging of two people is an impossibility, and where it seems to exist, it is a hemming-in, a mutual consent that robs one party or both parties of their fullest freedom and development. But once the realization is accepted that even between the closest people infinite distances exist, a marvelous living side-by-side can grow up for them, if they succeed in loving the expanse between them, which gives them the possibility of always seeing each other as a whole and before an immense sky.

That is why this too must be the criterion for rejection or choice: whether you are willing to stand guard over someone else's solitude, and whether you are able to set this same person at the gate of your own depths, which he learns of only through what steps forth, in holiday clothing, out of the great darkness.

Life is self-transformation, and human relationships, which are an extract of life, are the most changeable of all, they rise and fall from minute to minute, and lovers are those for whom no moment is like any another. People between whom nothing habitual ever takes place, nothing that has already existed, but just what is new, unexpected, unprecedented. There are such connections, which must be a very great, an almost unbearable happiness, but they can occur only between very rich beings, between those who have become, each for his own sake, rich, calm, and concentrated; only if two worlds are wide and deep and individual can they be combined.—Young people, it is obvious, can't achieve a connection like this, but if they understand their lives correctly, they can slowly grow up to such happiness and prepare themselves for it. When they love, they must not forget that they are beginners, bunglers of life, apprentices in love—they must *learn* love, and that (like all learning) takes calm, patience, and composure.

To take love seriously and to undergo it and learn it like a profession,— that is what young people need to do. Like so many other things, people have also misunderstood the position love has in life; they have made it into play and pleasure because they thought that play and pleasure are more blissful than work; but there is nothing happier than work, and love, precisely because it is the supreme happiness, can be nothing other than work.—So those who love must try to act as if they had a great work to accomplish: they must be much alone and go into themselves and gather and concentrate themselves; they must work; they must become something.

For the more we are, the richer everything we experience is. And those who want to have a deep love in their lives must collect and save for it, and gather honey.

RAINER MARIA RILKE
translated by Stephen Mitchell

from *The Courtship of Inanna and Dumuzi*

Inanna sang:
  "He has sprouted; he has burgeoned;
  He is lettuce planted by the water.
  He is the one my womb loves best.

  My well-stocked garden of the plain,
  My barley growing high in its furrow,
  My apple tree which bears fruit up to its crown,
  He is lettuce planted by the water.

  My honey-man, my honey-man sweetens me always.
  My lord, the honey-man of the gods,
  He is the one my womb loves best.
  His hand is honey, his foot is honey,
  He sweetens me always.

  My eager impetuous caresser of the navel,
  My caresser of the soft thighs,
  He is the one my womb loves best,
  He is lettuce planted by the water."

Dumuzi sang:
  "O Lady, your breast is your field.
  Inanna, your breast is your field.
  Your broad field pours out plants.
  Your broad field pours out grain.
  Water flows from on high for your servant.
  Bread flows from on high for your servant.
  Pour it out for me, Inanna.
  I will drink all you offer."

Inanna sang:
   "Make your milk sweet and thick, my bridegroom.
   My shepherd, I will drink your fresh milk.
   Wild bull, Dumuzi, make your milk sweet and thick.

   I will drink your fresh milk.

   Let the milk of the goat flow in my sheepfold.
   Fill my holy churn with honey cheese.
   Lord Dumuzi, I will drink your fresh milk.

   My husband, I will guard my sheepfold for you.
   I will watch over your house of life, the storehouse,
   The shining quivering place which delights Sumer—
   The house which decides the fates of the land,
   The house which gives the breath of life to the people.
   I, the queen of the palace, will watch over your house."

Dumuzi spoke:
   "My sister, I would go with you to my garden.
   Inanna, I would go with you to my garden.
   I would go with you to my orchard.
   I would go with you to my apple tree.
   There I would plant the sweet, honey-covered seed."

Inanna spoke:
   "He brought me into his garden.
   My brother, Dumuzi, brought me into his garden.
   I strolled with him among the standing trees,
   I stood with him among the fallen trees,
   By an apple tree I knelt as is proper.
   Before my brother coming in song,
   Who rose to me out of the poplar leaves,
   Who came to me in the midday heat,

Before my lord Dumuzi,
I poured out plants from my womb,
I placed plants before him,
I poured out plants before him,
I placed grain before him,
I poured out grain before him,
I poured out grain from my womb."

Inanna sang:
"Last night as I, the queen, was shining bright,
Last night as I, the Queen of Heaven, was shining bright,
As I was shining bright and dancing,
Singing praises at the coming of the night—
He met me—he met me!
My lord Dumuzi met me.
He put his hand into my hand.
He pressed his neck close against mine.

My high priest is ready for the holy loins.
My lord Dumuzi is ready for the holy loins.
The plants and herbs in the field are ripe.
O Dumuzi! Your fullness is my delight!"

She called for it, she called for it, she called for the bed!
She called for the bed that rejoices the heart.
She called for the bed that sweetens the loins.
She called for the bed of kingship.
She called for the bed of queenship.
Inanna called for the bed:
"Let the bed that rejoices the heart be prepared!
Let the bed that sweetens the loins be prepared!
Let the bed of queenship be prepared!
Let the bed of kingship be prepared!
Let the royal bed be prepared!"
Inanna spread the bridal sheet across the bed.

She called to the king:
   "The bed is ready!"
   She called to her bridegroom:
   "The bed is waiting!"

He put his hand in her hand.
He put his hand to her heart.
Sweet is the sleep of hand-to-hand.
Sweeter still the sleep of heart-to-heart.

Inanna spoke:
   "I bathed for the wild bull,
   I bathed for the shepherd Dumuzi,
   I perfumed my sides with ointment,
   I coated my mouth with sweet-smelling amber,
   I painted my eyes with kohl.

   He shaped my loins with his fair hands,
   The shepherd Dumuzi filled my lap with cream and milk,
   He stroked my pubic hair,
   He watered my womb.
   He laid his hands on my holy vulva,
   He smoothed my black boat with cream,
   He quickened my narrow boat with milk,
   He caressed me on the bed.

   Now I will caress my high priest on the bed,
   I will caress the faithful shepherd Dumuzi,
   I will caress his loins, the shepherdship of the land,
   I will decree a sweet fate for him."

The king went with lifted head to the holy loins.
He went with lifted head to the loins of Inanna.
He went to the queen with lifted head.
He opened wide his arms to the holy priestess of heaven.

Inanna spoke:

   "My beloved, the delight of my eyes, met me.

   We rejoiced together.

   He took his pleasure of me.

   He brought me into his house.

   He laid me down on the fragrant honey-bed.

   My sweet love, lying by my heart,

   Tongue-playing, one by one,

   My fair Dumuzi did so fifty times.

   Now, my sweet love is sated.

   Now he says:

   'Set me free, my sister, set me free.

   You will be a little daughter to my father.

   Come, my beloved sister, I would go to the palace.

   Set me free . . .' "

Inanna spoke:

   "My blossom-bearer, your allure was sweet.

   My blossom-bearer in the apple orchard,

   My bearer of fruit in the apple orchard,

   Dumuzi-*abzu*, your allure was sweet.

   My fearless one,

   My holy statue,

   My statue outfitted with sword and lapis lazuli diadem,

   How sweet was your allure . . . . "

ANCIENT SUMERIAN
translated by Diane Wolkstein and Samuel Noah Kramer

"The texts translated here," Professor Kramer writes, "date back to 2000 B.C.E.
Female deities were worshiped amd adored all through Sumerian history, but the
goddess who outweighed, overshadowed, and outlasted them all was a deity known
to the Sumerians by the name of Inanna, "Queen of Heaven," and to the Semites
who lived in Sumer by the name of Ishtar. Inanna played a greater role in myth,
epic, and hymn than any other deity, male or female."

from *Forms of the Implicit Love of God*

When one human being is attached to another by a bond of affection that contains any degree of necessity, it is impossible that he should wish autonomy to be preserved both in himself and in the other. Impossible by virtue of the mechanism of nature. But possible by the miraculous intervention of the supernatural. This miracle is friendship.

"Friendship is an equality made of harmony," said the Pythagoreans. There is harmony because there is a supernatural oneness between two opposites, necessity and freedom, the two opposites that God combined in creating the world and men. There is equality because each wants to preserve the faculty of free consent both in himself and in the other.

When anyone wishes to subordinate himself to another human being or consents to be subordinated to him, there is no trace of friendship. There is no friendship where there is inequality.

A friendship is soiled as soon as necessity prevails, even for one moment, over the desire to preserve the faculty of free consent in oneself and in the other. In all human things, necessity is the principle of impurity. All friendship is impure if even a trace of the desire to please or the contrary desire is found in it. In a perfect friendship these two desires are completely absent. The two friends fully consent to be two and not one, they respect the distance which the fact of being two distinct creatures places between them. Man has the right to desire to be in direct union with God alone.

Friendship is the miracle by which one human being consents to view from a distance, and without coming nearer, the very being who is as necessary to him as food. It is the strength of soul that Eve didn't have; and yet she didn't need the fruit. If she had been hungry at the moment when she looked at the fruit, and if in spite of that she had remained indefinitely looking at it without taking one step toward it, she would have performed a miracle analogous to that of perfect friendship.

Through this supernatural power of respect for human autonomy, friendship is very similar to the pure forms of compassion and gratitude aroused by affliction. In both cases the opposites that are the terms of the harmony are necessity and freedom, or in other words subordination and equality. These two pairs of opposites are equivalent.

From the fact that the desire to please and the contrary desire are absent in pure friendship, it has in it, along with affection, something like complete indifference. Although it is a bond between two people, it has something impersonal about it. It doesn't destroy impartiality. It doesn't in any way prevent us from imitating the perfection of the heavenly Father who everywhere sends the sunlight and the rain. On the contrary, friendship and this imitation are a mutual condition of each other, at least usually. For as almost every human being is joined to others by bonds of affection that contain some degree of necessity, he can't approach perfection except by transforming this affection into friendship. Friendship has something universal about it. It consists in loving a human being as we would like to be able to love every particular one of those who make up the human race. Just as a geometrician looks at one particular figure in order to deduce the universal properties of the triangle, someone who knows how to love directs upon a particular human being a universal love. The consent to preserve autonomy in ourselves and in others is in its essence something universal. As soon as we desire this preservation in more than one single being, we desire it in all beings; for we stop arranging the order of the world in a circle around a center that is here below. We transport the center of the circle above the heavens.

Friendship doesn't have this power if the two beings who love each other, through an illegitimate use of affection, think that they are only one. But in that case there is also no friendship in the true sense of the word. That is, so to speak, an adulterous union, even when it happens between two married people. Friendship exists only where distance is preserved and respected.

The simple fact of having pleasure in thinking about anything in the same way as the beloved person does, or in any case the fact of desiring such an agreement of opinions, is an attack upon the purity of the friendship as well as upon its intellectual integrity. That is very frequent. But a pure friendship is rare.

Pure friendship is an image of the original and perfect friendship that is the very essence of God. It is impossible for two human beings to be one while scrupulously respecting the distance that separates them, unless God is present in each of them. The point where parallels meet is infinity.

SIMONE WEIL
translated by Stephen Mitchell

Simone Weil (1909–1943) was the most profound modern Western theologian. This passage contains some essential truths about marriage, which is the supreme instance of friendship. (Weil's gnosticism can be distracting, so please disregard her contrast between "natural" and "supernatural," and between "here below" and "above the heavens.")

    S. M.

CEREMONIES

Preface

Here, for you to think about, are some traditional and non-traditional American wedding ceremonies. As you read them, thinking about what you want to do with your own ceremony, it is probably useful to pay attention to their main elements.

Most of the Christian ceremonies, and most non-traditional ceremonies, have more or less the same structure:

1. AN OPENING PRAYER OR INVOCATION, which addresses and in a way creates the community of value and the sacred space in which the wedding occurs.

2. THE INTERROGATION, in which the celebrant asks the couple publicly if they are entering on the vows of their own free will; the congregation is also sometimes addressed (this is the moment, in old movies, when the minister asks if there is any reason why this wedding should not go forward and just then the real groom, Clark Gable or Cary Grant, shows up).

3. THE PRESENTATION, or giving of the bride and groom to each other by their families, or families and friends. This is a survival of the old ritual of the giving of the bride to the husband by the father; it can be omitted, or adapted in various ways. To us this part of the ceremony makes a certain psychological sense, but if the family of the bride gives the bride away, the family of the groom should also give the groom away, one would think; in some rites the presentation comes before the interrogation.

4. THE VOWS, which are the marriage proper; this is the moment, in Christian ceremonies, when the bride and groom marry each other, and these are the words that bind them.

5. THE BLESSING AND EXCHANGE OF RINGS, which in the Jewish tradition is when the marriage occurs; that is, for the marriage to be valid, the groom gives the bride some object of value and she accepts it—that is the marriage. Christian ceremonies seem to have borrowed this beautiful ritual from the Jewish tradition, but in the Christian ceremony the exchange of rings is a symbol of the marriage which has already occurred in the spoken vows.

6. THE NUPTIAL BLESSING, which is the final prayer or prayers; it is also an evocation of the community of value and it gives the couple and their marriage back to their community after the private moment of the wedding, which is between the two of them.

And, finally, 7. THE KISS, also called the "salute" or "greeting" in some of the prim, older services; it is a favorite moment and it symbolizes, of course, the sexual bonding, which was thought to be the central, and seems always to have been a much-appreciated, event in the ancient ceremonies. For us, I think, it symbolizes romantic love, and it is an occasion for murmurs of pleasure and for applause; that clapping, like the clapping at the end of a comedy, is the symbol of communal delight.

The processions in and out of the sacred space in which the wedding occurs are also part of the ritual; they also have their symbolic meanings, and you will want to think about them. The procession into the church is a procession out of the family; the procession out of the church is a procession into a community that has been re-formed by the marriage. And then, in that new world, there is, in almost all cultures, a feast.

Inside this structure it can be seen that there are really three parts: the creation in language of the mythic or sacred space in which the marriage occurs, the act of marrying, and a giving of the marriage to the community as an expression of joy. In other words, the cosmic surround, the personal and spiritual center, and then the social world. This in turn suggests three places in the ceremony where kinds of poems might be appropriate: at the beginning, poems that express the meaning of the event; in the center, poems that address the meaning of the vow and of human love; and comic or celebratory poems at the end.

As you see, there is a wisdom in the shape of the ritual as it has been handed down to us. Inside it you can combine the words and symbols and ritual gestures that express what you want to express. It is something like making your own poem.

R. H.

Note: The Zen ceremony included here contains wedding vows, but it is interesting to note that the traditional Zen ceremony does not. The bride and groom simply recite what all Zen students recite, the vows known as the Threefold Refuge and the Thirteen Precepts. There is no special pledge of the one person to the other. Afterwards bride and groom light an altar candle together. Then there is an exchange of prayer beads and of rings. Philosophically, this is interesting because it is really outside the tradition of romantic bonding and of magical ceremony. It assumes that there is really only the one human task and the one set of vows. This is reflected in the words spoken by a priest at the beginning of the ceremony: ". . . you should give up your small selves and take refuge in each other, and to truly take refuge in each other means you should take refuge in all things. This is to live together and practice together."

This suggests a quite radical alternative to our present vows. A couple might simply want to say: "I vow to make every effort to live in awareness. I vow to live to benefit all beings"—because, in fact, they think there is no other vow to be made than words like these.

A Protestant Ceremony

The celebrant, facing the people and the persons to be married, with the woman to the right and the man to the left, addresses the congregation and says:

Dearly beloved: We have come together in the presence of God to witness and bless the joining together of this man and this woman in Holy Matrimony. The bond and covenant of marriage was established by God in creation, and our Lord Jesus Christ adorned this manner of life by his presence and first miracle at a wedding in Cana of Galilee. It signifies to us the mystery of the union between Christ and his Church, and Holy Scripture commends it to be honored among all people.

The union of husband and wife in heart, body, and mind is intended by God for their mutual joy; for the help and comfort given each other in prosperity and adversity; and, when it is God's will, for the procreation of children and their nurture in the knowledge and love of the Lord. Therefore marriage is not to be entered into unadvisedly or lightly, but reverently, deliberately, and in accordance with the purposes for which it was instituted by God.

THE INTERROGATION

Into this union _____ and _____ now come to be joined. If any of you can show just cause why they may not lawfully be married, speak now; or else for ever hold your peace.

Then the celebrant says to the persons to be married:
I require and charge you both, here in the presence of God, that if either of you know any reason why you may not be united in marriage lawfully, and in accordance with God's Word, you do now confess it.

The celebrant says to the woman:
_____ , will you have this man to be your husband; to live together in the covenant of marriage? Will you love him, comfort him, honor and keep

him, in sickness and in health; and, forsaking all others, be faithful to him as long as you both shall live?

The woman answers:
I will.

The celebrant says to the man:
_____ , will you have this woman to be your wife; to live together in the covenant of marriage? Will you love her, comfort her, honor and keep her, in sickness and in health; and, forsaking all others, be faithful to her as long as you both shall live?

The man answers:
I will.

The celebrant then addresses the congregation, saying:
Will all of you witnessing these promises do all in your power to uphold these two persons in their marriage?

People:
We will.

THE PRESENTATION

If there is to be a presentation of a giving in marriage, it takes place at this time. A hymn, psalm, or anthem may follow.

THE VOWS

The man, facing the woman and taking her right hand in his, says:
In the name of God, I, _____ , take you, _____ , to be my wife, to have and to hold from this day forward, for better for worse, for richer for poorer, in sickness and in health, to love and to cherish, until we are parted by death. This is my solemn vow.

Then they loose their hands, and the woman, still facing the man, takes his right hand in hers, and says:

In the name of God, I, _____ , take you, _____ , to be my husband, to have and to hold from this day forward, for better for worse, for richer for poorer, in sickness and in health, to love and to cherish, until we are parted by death. This is my solemn vow.

They loose their hands.

THE BLESSING AND EXCHANGE OF RINGS

The celebrant may ask God's blessing on a ring or rings, as follows:
Bless, O Lord, this ring [these rings] to be a sign of the vows by which this man and this woman have bound themselves to each other; through Jesus Christ our Lord.

People:
Amen.

The giver places the ring on the ring-finger of the other's hand and says:
_____ , I give you this ring as a symbol of my vow, and with all that I am, and all that I have, I honor you, in the Name of the Father, and of the Son, and of the Holy Spirit [*or* in the Name of God].

Then the celebrant joins the right hands of husband and wife and says:
Now that _____ and _____ have given themselves to each other by solemn vows, with the joining of hands and the giving and receiving of a ring [rings], I pronounce that they are husband and wife, in the Name of the Father, and of the Son, and of the Holy Spirit [*or* in the Name of God].
Those whom God has joined together let no one put asunder.

People:
Amen.

CONCLUDING PRAYERS

All standing, the celebrant says:
Let us pray together in the words our Savior taught us.

People and celebrant:

Our Father, who art in heaven, hallowed be thy Name. Thy kingdom come, thy will be done, on earth as it is in heaven. Give us this day our daily bread. And forgive us our trespasses, as we forgive those who trespass against us. And lead us not into temptation, but deliver us from evil. For thine is the kingdom, and the power, and the glory, for ever and ever. Amen.

The deacon or other person appointed reads the following prayers, to which the people respond, saying, Amen:

Let us pray.

Eternal God, creator and preserver of all life, author of salvation, and giver of grace: Look with favor upon the world you have made, and for which your Son gave his life, and especially upon this man and this woman whom you make one flesh in Holy Matrimony. *Amen.*

Give them wisdom and devotion in the ordering of their common life, that each may be to the other a strength in need, a counselor in perplexity, a comfort in sorrow, and a companion in joy. *Amen.*

Grant that their wills may be so knit together in your will, and their spirits in your spirit, that they may grow in love and peace with you and with each other all the days of their life. *Amen.*

Give them grace, when they hurt each other, to recognize and acknowledge their fault, and to seek each other's forgiveness and yours. *Amen.*

Make their life together a sign of Christ's love to this suffering and broken world, that unity may overcome estrangement, forgiveness heal guilt, and joy conquer despair. *Amen.*

Bestow on them, if it is your will, the gift and heritage of children, and the grace to bring them up to know you, to love you, and to serve you. *Amen.*

Give them such fulfillment of their mutual affection that they may reach out in love and concern for others. *Amen.*

Grant that all married persons who have witnessed these vows may find their lives strengthened and their loyalties confirmed. *Amen.*

Grant that the bonds of our common humanity, by which all your children are united to one another, and the living to the dead, may be so transformed by your grace, that your will may be done on earth as it is in heaven; where, O Father, with your Son and the Holy Spirit, you live and reign in perfect unity, now and for ever. *Amen.*

The people remain standing. The husband and wife kneel, and the celebrant says one of the following prayers:
Most gracious God, we give you thanks for your tender love in sending Jesus Christ to come among us, to be born of a human mother, and to make the way of the cross to be the way of life. We thank you, also, for consecrating the union of man and woman in his Name. By the power of your Holy Spirit, pour out the abundance of your blessing upon this man and this woman. Lead them into all peace. Let their love for each other be a seal upon their hearts, a mantle about their shoulders, and a crown upon their foreheads. Bless them in their work and in their companionship; in their sleeping and in their waking; in their joys and in their sorrows; in their life and in their death. Finally, in your mercy, bring them to that table where your saints feast for ever in your heavenly home; through Jesus Christ our Lord, who with you and the Holy Spirit lives and reigns, one God, now and for ever. *Amen.*

Or this:
O God, you have so consecrated the covenant of marriage that in it is represented the spiritual unity between Christ and his Church: Send therefore your blessing upon these your servants, that they may so love, honor, and cherish each other in faithfulness and patience, in wisdom and true godliness, that their home may be a haven of blessing and peace; through Jesus Christ our Lord, who with you and the Holy Spirit lives and reigns, one God, now and for ever. *Amen.*

The husband and wife still kneeling, the celebrant adds this blessing:
God the Father, God the Son, God the Holy Spirit, bless, preserve, and keep you; the Lord mercifully with his favor look upon you, and fill you with all

spiritual benediction and grace; that you may faithfully live together in this life, and in the age to come have life everlasting. *Amen.*

The celebrant may say to the people:
The peace of the Lord be always with you.

People:
And also with you.

The newly married couple then greet each other, after which greetings may be exchanged throughout the congregation.

THE BOOK OF COMMON PRAYER (1928)

A Catholic Ceremony

Priest:

My dear friends, you have come together in this church so that the Lord may seal and strengthen your love in the presence of the Church's minister and this community. Christ abundantly blesses this love. He has already consecrated you in baptism and now he enriches and strengthens you by a special sacrament, so that you may assume the duties of marriage in mutual and lasting faithfulness.

THE CONSENT

And so, in the presence of the Church, I ask you to state your intentions.
_____ and _____, have you come here freely and without reservation to give yourselves to each other in marriage?

Will you love and honor each other as husband and wife for the rest of your lives?

Will you accept children lovingly from God, and bring them up according to the law of Christ and his Church?

Each answers the questions separately.

The Priest then invites the couple to declare their consent:
Since it is your intention to enter into marriage, join your right hands and declare your consent before God and his Church.

The bride and the groom join hands.

THE VOWS

Groom:

I, _____, take you, _____, to be my wife. I promise to be true to you in good times and in bad, in sickness and in health. I will love and honor you all the days of my life.

Bride:

I, _____ , take you, _____ , to be my husband. I promise to be true to you in good times and in bad, in sickness and in health. I will love and honor you all the days of my life.

Priest:

You have declared your consent before the Church. May the Lord in his goodness strengthen your consent and fill you both with his blessings.

What God has joined, men must not divide.

People:

Amen.

THE BLESSING AND EXCHANGE OF RINGS

Priest:

May the Lord bless these rings which you give to each other as the sign of your love and faithfulness.

People:

Amen.

Groom (placing the ring on his wife's ring finger):

_____ , take this ring as a sign of my love and faithfulness. In the name of the Father, and of the Son, and of the Holy Spirit.

Bride (placing the ring on her husband's ring finger):

_____ , take this ring as a sign of my love and faithfulness. In the name of the Father, and of the Son, and of the Holy Spirit.

THE NUPTIAL BLESSING

Priest:

My dear friends, let us turn to the Lord and pray that he will bless with his grace _____ and _____ , now married in Christ, and that he will unite in love the couple he has joined in this holy bond.

Father, by your power you have made everything out of nothing. In the beginning you created the universe and made mankind in your own likeness. You gave man the constant help of woman so that man and woman should no longer be two, but one flesh, and you teach us that what you have united may never be divided.

Look with love upon this woman, your daughter, now joined to her husband in marriage. She asks your blessing. Give her the grace of love and peace. May she always follow the example of the holy women whose praises are sung in the scriptures. May her husband put his trust in her and recognize that she is his equal and the heir with him to the life of grace. May he always honor her and love her as Christ loves his bride, the Church.

Father, keep them always true to your commandments. Keep them faithful in marriage, and let them be living examples of Christian life.

Give them the strength which comes from the Gospel, so that they may be witnesses of Christ to others.

[Bless them with children and help them to be good parents. May they live to see their children's children.] *This paragraph may be omitted whenever circumstances suggest it; if, for example, the couple are past child-bearing age.*

And, after a happy old age, grant them fullness of life with the saints in heaven.

We ask this through Christ our Lord.

People:
Amen.

THE CONCLUSION

Priest:
May [your children bless you,] your friends console you, and all people live in peace with you.

People:
Amen.

Priest:

May you always bear witness to the love of God in this world, so that the afflicted and the needy will find in you generous friends, and welcome you into the joys of heaven.

People:

Amen.

Priest:

And may almighty God bless you all, the Father, and the Son, and the Holy Spirit.

People:

Amen.

THE RITE OF MARRIAGE

A Jewish Ceremony

Blessed be you who come in the name of the Lord; we bless you from the house of the Lord.

Come, let us bow in worship; let us kneel before the God who made us.

Serve the Unnamable with joy; enter God's presence with gladness.

PSALM 100 *(see page 37)*.

May the One who is powerful above all beings, blessed through all beings, and great within all beings, bless the bride and the groom.

Poem

The blessing is recited over a cup of wine:
Blessed are you, Unnamable God, source of the universe, who created the fruit of the vine.

Blessed are you, Unnamable God, source of the universe, who purify us with your commandments and give us marriage as a path to you. Blessed are you, Unnamable God, who give us the mystery of marriage.

The bride and groom drink from the first cup of wine.

The groom places the ring on the forefinger of the bride's right hand and says:
Now, by this ring, you are consecrated to me, according to the Law of Moses and of Israel.

If there is a Marriage Contract (ketubah), *it is now read by the rabbi or celebrant, and the following Seven Benedictions are recited over the second cup of wine:*
Blessed are you, Unnamable God, source of the universe, who created the fruit of the vine.

Blessed are you, Unnamable God, source of the universe, who created all things in your glory.

Blessed are you, Unnamable God, source of the universe, creator of woman and man.

Blessed are you, Unnamable God, source of the universe, who created woman and man in your image and placed eternity in their hearts. Blessed are you, Unnamable God, creator of woman and man.

May Zion rejoice and exult, as her children are gathered inside her. Blessed are you, Unnamable God, source of the universe, who fill Zion with joy at the return of her children.

Give joy to these two loving friends, as you gave joy to the first man and woman in the garden of Eden. Blessed are you, Unnamable God, who give joy to the bride and the groom.

Blessed are you, Unnamable God, source of the universe, who created happiness and joy, bride and groom, gladness, exhilaration, pleasure, and delight, love and friendship, harmony and peace. Unnamable God, may there soon be heard in the cities of Israel and in the streets of Jerusalem, the sound of joy and the sound of happiness, the sound of Jew and Arab living in harmony, the sound of the bride and the sound of the groom, the jubilant sound of lovers joined under the wedding canopy, and of young people feasting and singing. Blessed are you, Unnamable God, who wish bride and groom to fill each other with joy.

The bride and groom drink from the second cup of wine.

The groom breaks a glass by stepping on it

The rabbi or celebrant recites the Benediction:
May the Unnamable bless you and keep you.

May the Unnamable make his face shine upon you and be gracious to you.

May the Unnamable let you feel his presence within you and give you peace.

THE TRADITIONAL WEDDING SERVICE
adapted by Stephen Mitchell

A Non-Theistic Judeo-Christian Ceremony

Entrance March.
The celebrant takes his or her place.
The groom and the best man take their places.
Procession of the bridal party.

Celebrant:
Dearly beloved, we are gathered here in the presence of these witnesses, to join together this man and this woman in holy matrimony; which is an honorable estate, instituted in antiquity and revered since time immemorial as the noblest and most tender of human relationships. It is therefore not to be entered into unadvisedly, but reverently and discreetly. Into this holy estate these two persons come now to be joined.

I ask you both, as you stand in the presence of your families and friends, to remember that love and loyalty alone will avail as the foundation of a happy and enduring home. No other human ties are more tender, no other vows more sacred than those that you now assume. If these solemn vows are kept inviolate, and if you steadfastly endeavor to live according to the best that is within you, your life together will be full of joy, and the home that you are establishing will abide in peace.

Celebrant to the groom:
_____ , will you have this woman to be your wedded wife, to live together in the estate of matrimony? Will you love her, comfort her, honor and keep her, in sickness and in health; and forsaking all others keep only to her as long as you both shall live?

Groom:
I will.

Celebrant to the bride:

————, will you have this man to be your wedded husband, to live together in the estate of matrimony? Will you love him, comfort him, honor and keep him, in sickness and in health; and forsaking all others keep only to him as long as you both shall live?

Bride:
I will.

Celebrant:
Who presents this woman to be married to this man?

Bride's father.
I do.

The celebrant takes the bride's right hand from her father and places it in the groom's right hand. The groom repeats after the celebrant:
I, ————, take you, ————, to be my wedded wife, to have and to hold, from this day forward, for better for worse, for richer for poorer, in sickness and in health, to love and to cherish, till death do us part. This I solemnly vow.

The celebrant loosens their hands. The bride takes the groom's right hand in her right hand and repeats after the celebrant:
I, ————, take you, ————, to be my wedded husband, to have and to hold, from this day forward, for better for worse, for richer for poorer, in sickness and in health, to love and to cherish, till death do us part. This I solemnly vow.

They loosen their hands.
The best man and the bridesmaid give the celebrant the rings.

Celebrant:

These rings are an outward and visible sign of an inward love, signifying to all the uniting of this man and this woman in holy matrimony.

The celebrant gives one ring to the groom, who puts it on the third finger of the bride's left hand. Holding the ring there, he repeats after the celebrant:
In token and pledge of the vow made between us, with this ring I marry you.

The celebrant gives the other ring to the bride, who puts it on the third finger of the groom's left hand. Holding the ring there, she repeats after the celebrant:
In token and pledge of the vow made between us, with this ring I marry you.

Celebrant:

As by these rings you symbolize your marriage bond, may their meaning sink into your hearts and bind your lives together by devotion and faithfulness to one another. In mutual self-consecration and in ever-deepening love for each other, may you establish a home filled with the spirit of faith, truth, and goodness.

The celebrant joins their right hands together and with his right hand on theirs says:
Forasmuch as _____ and _____ have consented together in holy wedlock, and have witnessed this before this company, and have made solemn vows to each other and have declared this by joining hands and by giving and receiving a ring, I pronounce that they are husband and wife together.

May all blessings attend you,
May joy pervade your lives together,
May your home be forever a place of peace and true fulfillment.

Embrace.
Recessional.

THE BOOK OF COMMON PRAYER
adapted by Huston Smith

A Zen Ceremony

Music.
Entrance.

Three bells. Offering of incense and bows. The celebrant lights a large white candle, which symbolizes the Source.

A few moments of silence.

Candlelighting ceremony. The bride and the groom, each holding a small candle, approach the Source-candle and bow. First the bride, then the groom, light their candles from the Source-candle and leave them on the altar. This symbolizes the illumination of their hearts from the source of light.

Celebrant:
We have come together for the marriage of _____ and _____ . May they continue to deepen their life with each other and with all sentient beings.

Marriage begins in the giving of words. We cannot join ourselves to one another without giving our word. And this must be an unconditional giving, for in joining ourselves to one another we join ourselves to the unknown.

May I extend my joy to you on this happy occasion. _____ and _____ , you are about to take a new step forward into life. This day is made possible not only because of your love for each other, but through the grace of your parents and of the whole society. It is my hope that your fulfillment and joy in each other and in yourselves will increase with every passing year.

Poem

Celebrant:

Courtesy and consideration even in anger and adversity are the seeds of compassion. Love is the fruit of compassion. Trust, love, and respect are the sustaining virtues of marriage. They enable us to learn from each situation, and help us to realize that everywhere we turn we meet ourself.

The celebrant takes a small bowl of water and, with a leaf, flicks a drop of wisdom water onto the bride and groom.

Celebrant:

We nourish ourselves and each other in living by the following five precepts:

1. In every way we can, we allow our deepest Self to appear.
2. We take full responsibility for our own life, in all its infinite dimensions.
3. We affirm our trust in the honesty and wisdom of our own body, which with our love and reverence always shows us the true way.
4. We are committed to embrace all parts of ourself, including our deepest fears and shadows, so that they can be transformed into light.
5. We affirm our willingness to keep our heart open, even in the midst of great pain.

Poem

Celebrant:

Now _____ and _____ will take their marriage vows.

Bride:

I, _____, take you, _____, to be my husband, in equal love, as a mirror for my true Self, as a partner on my path, to honor and to cherish, in sorrow and in joy, till death do us part.

Groom:

I, _____, take you, _____, to be my wife, in equal love, as a mirror for my true Self, as a partner on my path, to honor and to cherish, in sorrow and in joy, till death do us part.

Poem

Exchange of rings

Celebrant:
Now _____ and _____ celebrate their love and proclaim their union with rings of precious metal. The precious nature of their rings represents the subtle and wonderful essence they find by losing themselves in each other, and the subtle and wonderful essence they find individually, through their mutual love, respect, and support. The metal itself represents the long life they may cultivate together, not only in years, but in all the infinite dimensions of each moment they share.

Signing of documents.

As the music begins, the celebrant strews fresh rosepetals over the bride and groom and over the whole congregation.

Exit.

ZEN CENTER OF SAN FRANCISCO; DIAMOND SANGHA
adapted by Vicki Chang

A Zen-Unitarian-Catholic-American-Transcendentalist Ceremony

This is the text of a wedding ceremony performed for a young couple who grew up in northern California and chose to be married outdoors on a bluff overlooking Tomales Bay. They wanted a ceremony partly traditional and partly written for themselves out of the things they wanted to say to each other and to their friends. They collaborated with a minister in the creation of the following service which blends a traditional service with personal elements.

Music. Processional.

ADDRESS TO THE CONGREGATION

Celebrant:

We are gathered in this beautiful place to witness the joining of _____ and _____ in marriage. They particularly wanted to invite you here because their sense of spirituality and the growth of their love is connected to this place. They've come here many mornings like this one and walked quietly, looking at birds, at wildflowers, at the wind on the bay, and the hills in the distance. It's given them a feeling of timelessness and peace, and a sense of connectedness to life. They've learned here that falling in love with another person and getting to know them is a little like the exploration of a wild and lovely place, and that loving another person can deepen your sense of connectedness to all of life. And that the intimacy and the surprises of that experience are a form of reverence and can be a form of wholeness. And it is this that they wanted to share with you on the day of their wedding.

A wedding ceremony is an outward form. To be true, it must be a symbol of something inner and real: a sacred personal union which nature might mirror, a church solemnize, or a state declare legal, but which only love can create and mutual loyalty fulfill.

To last, the marriage of these two must be a consecration of each to the other, and of both to the wider community of which they are a part.

For the first reading, _____ and _____ have chosen a poem by
_____ .

First Reading

PRESENTING OF THE BRIDE AND GROOM

Celebrant:
Who presents the bride in marriage?

Bride's Family:
We do.

Celebrant:
Who presents the bridegroom in marriage?

Groom's Family:
We do.

[Alternative version, since "presents" is a lukewarm substitute for the old question: Who gives this woman?]
Celebrant:
Who gives the bride in marriage?

Bride's Family:
She gives herself,
and we share her giving, joyfully.

Celebrant:
Who gives the bridegroom in marriage?

Groom's Family:
He gives himself,
and we share his giving, joyfully.

INTERROGATION

Celebrant to Groom:

_____ , will you have this woman to be your wife, to live together in the holy estate of marriage? Will you love her, comfort her, honor and keep her, in sickness and in health, in sorrow and in joy, and be faithful to her, as long as you both shall live?

Groom:
I will.

Celebrant to Bride:

_____ , will you have this man to be your husband, to live together in the holy estate of marriage? Will you love him, comfort him, honor and keep him, in sickness and in health, in sorrow and in joy, and be faithful to him, as long as you both shall live?

Bride:
I will.

Celebrant:
The second reading, a poem by _____ , was selected by _____ and she (he) will read it for them now.

Second Reading

THE MARRIAGE PLEDGE

Celebrant:

_____ and _____ , it's time to say the pledges which will marry you. Please face each other.

Groom:
I, _____ , take you, _____ , to be my wife, to be the mother of my children, to be the companion of my heart, to have and to hold, from this day

forward, for better for worse, for richer for poorer, in sickness and in health, to love and to cherish, till death do us part.

Bride:
I, _____ , take you, _____ , to be my husband, to be the father of my children, to be the companion of my heart, to have and to hold, from this day forward, for better for worse, for richer for poorer, in sickness and in health, to love and to cherish, till death do us part.

Celebrant:
Will you who witness these pledges do your utmost to support this marriage?

Congregation:
We will.

RING CEREMONY
Celebrant:
Rings are an ancient symbol, blessed and simple. Round like the sun, like the eye, like arms that embrace. Circles, for love that is given comes back round again and again. Therefore, may these symbols remind you that your love, like the sun, illumines; that your love, like the eye, must see clearly; and that your love, like arms that embrace, is a grace upon this world.

Groom
_____ , with this ring I thee wed.

Bride
_____ , with this ring I thee wed.

At this point the celebrant may want to read a prayer of his or her choosing.

Celebrant:

The final reading was chosen by _____ and _____ to express something of their feeling about this occasion, and it will be read by _____ .

Third Reading

Celebrant:

_____ and _____ have chosen each other from the many men and women of the earth, have declared their love and purpose before this gathering, and have made their pledge each to the other symbolized by the holding of hands and the giving and receiving of rings. Therefore, I declare that they are husband and wife.

Let all others honor them and the threshold of their house. May they carry into their marriage the beauty and the tranquility of this place, and keep in it always the sense of exploration and the peace and intimacy they have shared here, which is symbolized in the name of this beach: heart's desire.

May they find here the good beginning of their married life and the fruitfulness of many years.

THE WEDDING KISS

Recessional Music

JAMES FORD, WITH LEIF HASS AND MARGARET HANDLEY

The Tao of Marriage

The deepest intimacy with the beloved becomes possible when we have experienced intimacy with the self. Intimacy with the self means awakening to our true nature. The old Zen stories say, about the moment of a Master's enlightenment, "Suddenly he was intimate."

"Go deeper than love," D. H. Lawrence wrote, "for the soul has greater depths." The willingness to go deeper than love is itself a kind of love, a desire to meet the beloved beyond desire, in the darkness where there is no self, no other. For this meeting, a man and a woman must be whole enough in themselves to step out of themselves, into the place of mutual transformation. They are able to surrender everything they know, everything they love, with the abandon that a Master has at the hour of death. Transformation *is* a death. It is also a birth, and can be as painful as any physical birth. Painful or ecstatic, it requires a fundamental trust. "Into your hand I commit my spirit."

A man and a woman who enter this depth of intimacy find themselves standing in the garden where Adam and Eve stood. All things are possible for them. The ancient Chinese sage Tzu-ssu said, "For the mature person, the Tao begins in the relation between man and woman, and ends in the infinite vastness of the universe." They have traced their love for each other back to the root of love, the radiant non-self, the bodhisattva's serene compassion. Like the wedding ring, it has no beginning, no end.

STEPHEN MITCHELL

Acknowledgments

We want to thank Robert Baldock, Joan Baranow, Coleman Barks, Philip Barry, Dan Bellem, Samuel Bercholz, Richard Boeke, Alan Cheuse, Toi Derricote, Dan Gerber, Jane Hirshfield, Laura Jason, Kenneth Lincoln, Heather McHugh, Peter Nabokov, Jim Paul, Bill Simmons, Mona Simpson, Huston Smith, Gary Soto, and David Watts for their suggestions and advice. And we'd like to express our particular gratitude to Kristin Hass for many hours of research and lively criticism, and to Michael Katz, our agent, for taking such good care of this book.